P9-DOE-524

A Life of My Own

BY THE SAME AUTHOR

Each Day A New Beginning:
Daily Meditations for Women

A Life of My Own

*Meditations on
Hope and Acceptance*

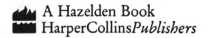
A Hazelden Book
HarperCollins*Publishers*

Interior design by Timothy Quinn McIndoo

A LIFE OF MY OWN: *Meditations on Hope and Acceptance.*
Copyright © 1993 by the Hazelden Foundation. This edition
published by arrangement with the Hazelden Foundation. All
rights reserved. Printed in the United States of America. No
part of this book may be used or reproduced in any manner
whatsoever without written permission except in the case of
brief quotations embodied in critical articles and reviews. For
information address HarperCollins Publishers, 10 East 53rd
Street, New York, NY 10022.

FIRST HARPERCOLLINS EDITION PUBLISHED IN 1993

Library of Congress Catalog Card Number
92–54662
ISBN 0–06–255287–2

93 94 95 96 97 BANTA 10 9 8 7 6 5 4 3 2 1

This edition is printed on acid-free paper that meets the
American National Standards Z39.48 Standard.

When we first heard the slogan <u>One Day at a Time</u>, it probably didn't mean much to us. But our program friends were quick to offer it as a solution to our incessant worrying about the future. Now we appreciate the relief that comes with living twenty-four hours at a time. It makes any situation manageable. Our fears about the future simply disappear, and when the future arrives, it too is manageable.

Today is what matters. The future isn't here yet.

Living just for today can still seem overwhelming if we forget to seek our Higher Power's help in our activities. That's the key to ultimate serenity. That we can live just for today with God's help is the program's most important message, one we have been chosen to receive. What lucky people we are.

LIVING IN THE PRESENT

T° GOD TRUSTING

My companion is God. Together we can figure out what I should do in every situation I face today.

With willingness and effort, we can turn our defects into assets.

DEFECTS of
OHARACTER

T² ASSETS

In the midst of a power struggle, we have a hard time comprehending that our controlling behavior can become an asset. Controlling behavior is not an asset if it is used only to intimidate others. However, using it to manage ourselves makes it an asset. Controlling our thoughts, our feelings, our actions, and our attitudes puts us in charge of who we are every moment, in every situation. It is empowering to realize that we can turn a damaging defect into a worthy asset.

Another troubling defect that we may want to work with is intolerance. Believing we are right seems so natural that it's mind-boggling to *truly* accept that another person's perception is as valid as our own. Without realizing it, we become trapped by our narrow viewpoint. But as with control, when we reach that point of acceptance, we discover freedom. Life becomes an adventure again.

It's human to have defects, but I can choose whether or not they control me. I can work to turn a defect into an asset today, if I choose to.

We can all recognize humble people when we see them: Martin Luther King, Jr., Mother Teresa, and Gandhi come quickly to mind. Even among our friends, we catch glimpses of humility every time they honestly seek guidance and God's will, admitting they lack the answers or the knowledge they need. It's not an accident that we see "humility in action." We are the students; they are our teachers.

Quieting our hearts and our minds to receive God's guidance relieves us of pressure we may not have realized was there. We grow used to carrying too many burdens, trying to control too many outcomes.

If we choose to be humble—that is, willing to give up our burdens to God—we will be in for difficult yet rewarding times: difficult in that we can no longer be sure events and people will turn out according to our plan; rewarding in that we can look forward to the best outcome for all concerned.

Being humble *means having a quiet heart.*

My quiet heart will feel God's presence today. My quiet mind will hear my directions.

"We admitted..."

ACCEPTANCE

We have many things to admit if we really want the help of the program. We have to admit we have tried to control far more than is ours to control. We have to admit our shortcomings to ourselves and to others. We have to admit we need to hear what others in the program want to share. We have to admit that we need a belief in a Higher Power for guidance and courage. We have to admit we have hurt others and need to make amends. Most of all, we have to admit we sincerely want better lives, ones with the joy and peace we deserve.

We won't be able to define our dreams for the future until we can clear our minds of the chaos of the past. The program will help us admit what we need to and accept what comes next. In a very short time, our vision for the future will resemble nothing from our past. Saner living and joy are expected.

Every time I admit the true nature of my behavior I am expressing my honest desire to find happiness. Today can be a new beginning for me.

The founders of Alcoholics Anonymous, Bill W. and Dr. Bob, knew from firsthand experience the value of telling someone else "what [it] used to be like, what happened, and what [it's] like now." They were graced with sobriety and maintained it as a result of their commitment to carrying their message to other people. Step Twelve asks us to follow their example.

Carrying the message is our answer too.

Our message is one of hope. Other people gave it to us when we entered the program, and we maintain hope by telling others how our lives have changed. Perhaps we need frequent reminders of the pain of our struggle to maintain appreciation for how good our lives have become. Being in the program certainly gives us the opportunities. Sharing our stories with others who are troubled helps us too. And if it's their time to accept help, others will gain hope from our stories.

I can keep my hope for a better life by giving hope to someone else today.

Life can be difficult when the people we care about are dependent on alcohol or other mood-altering chemicals. Fortunately, we have a pathway to freedom from the pain caused by alcoholism or other drug addiction. It's called Twelve Step recovery.

A Life of My Own may be your introduction to the philosophy that undergirds Twelve Step recovery. These daily meditations offer suggestions and guidelines for handling both the universal and the unique struggles in our lives *one day at a time.* These guidelines had their genesis in the program of Alcoholics Anonymous more than fifty years ago; now more than one hundred other Twelve Step programs, such as Al-Anon, Alateen, and Co-Dependents Anonymous, rely on these or similar guidelines. They have helped millions of people—men and women, young and old—find serenity.

The attainment of serenity may seem impossible to you right now, particularly if you feel as I felt when I first came into a Twelve Step program. Yet it is possible to feel better. After attending meetings for a while and listening to how others in the group have changed the patterns in their lives, you will note a change in your mood and attitude too.

We learn from each other. Sharing our experiences and hope and offering strength and support when friends need it to survive their struggles strengthen each of us to handle the bumps in our personal journey. We'll never be free of the bumps. They are part of life. But we can get free of our obsession to control the bumps in other people's lives.

The people we love may still be using chemicals; in fact, they may never quit. Still, we can learn to love and accept them anyway. More important, we can learn to let them live their own lives, while we learn to live only our own. It's particularly difficult to watch a son or daughter, a parent, or a spouse make a mess of his or her life. Alcohol and other drugs can do that all too quickly. Unfortunately, we can't stop it. We can't really help them unless they want help. We can help ourselves, however. That's why we are holding this book.

If someone has suggested that codependency is your problem, you will find help in these pages. If someone has labeled you as an "adult child," you will find help here. If focusing on the life of someone else, anyone else, consumes much of your attention, you too will find help here. A Twelve Step program, friends like the ones you'll get to know around the meeting tables, and a book like this one are your gateway to freedom from obsession with others and the pain that haunts you.

You aren't alone. Many of us travel this path with you. Together, all of us can discover the peace that we crave and deserve. Let's begin.

JANUARY

When our lives were wracked by our close association with people suffering from the disease of chemical dependency, we lost a sense of who we really were. Seeing ourselves through the behavior of others cancelled out our positive qualities, and our <u>self-esteem</u> plummeted.

Every human being brings something very special to the world.

The program, particularly the Steps, helps us regain the knowledge of who we are. And through that process we discover the qualities we have that we can share with others. The willingness to "take inventory" of our behavior, our thoughts, and our values is the place to begin.

Accepting that every individual is endowed with a special talent that is unique and necessary to the whole of humanity helps each of us, especially on the days we'd rather hide under the covers. We do have something to give everyone we meet today. How we thought of ourselves in the past as the result of the alcoholism around us can't block us any longer. We are free and our talents are needed.

Every situation I meet today will be affected by my presence. I have something to give that only I can give.

If we embody the principles taught in the Twelve Steps, our lives will get better.

Whether our first Twelve Step meeting was last week, last year, or five years ago, we all have one thing in common: We have discovered hope and our lives are getting better. The good feelings seem almost contagious. Perhaps they are. We have learned from other people's examples, and all of us have found life's pitfalls easier to navigate since we began relying on the slogans, the Steps, and the principles of the program.

Many of us came into this program quite certain that it wouldn't help us. Our troubles were far too serious. And some of us resisted the help that was immediately offered. It couldn't be that easy. Stewing a bit longer and hanging on to the pain were choices we made.

Now we are seeing newcomers who are like we were. It makes us joyful to know just how much we all have to look forward to.

How grateful I am that I gave up my resistance. My life will be as joyful as I make it today.

Most of us are no longer sure what we want to be doing a year or even a month from now. When we are called upon to make <u>decisions</u> that commit us to a certain path in the future, we shudder. Will we be allowed to change our minds?

No decision has to bind us forever.

What a change this is from earlier years. Many of us led very controlled lives. We felt safest when we knew exactly what we were going to do. We liked it best when we were able to control others' lives too, even though we failed at that much of the time.

Although we may have responsibilities at work and at home, we are so much freer now. And we can decide, moment by moment, what we *need* to do for ourselves. At first it feels irresponsible, not being responsible for everyone, changing our minds when we need to. However, we will grow into this new way of living. And we'll love it!

My decisions today will be for this day only. I can change my mind tomorrow.

_Turning
adversity
into
opportunity
is possible._

ATTITUDE

We didn't escape problems just because we came to a Twelve Step program. Problems still exist, whether it's a car that won't run, a neighbor who complains, a spiteful co-worker, or family member who drinks or uses other drugs.

The difference is, now we can keep these situations in perspective. No problem means the end of the world. Before, even the smallest of problems sometimes devastated us.

Through listening to old-timers, we are beginning to realize that every situation offers us a unique opportunity to respond in more thoughtful, loving ways. Without this program, we might never have learned that having problems is the path to the growth and serenity we all seek. Now we turn to God for guidance, and through our trust in God we see the problem transformed into an opportunity. To acknowledge life as being filled with opportunity rather than problems is a tiny shift in perspective that gives us huge rewards.

I will look for my opportunities today. My Higher Power will show me how to handle them. My reward will be growth.

From our first introduction to other men and women who have faced firsthand the illness of chemical dependency, we sense the spirit of hope in their words and in their faces. Some of us have had little or no hope for many years. It's no wonder we initially doubt that our lives can change. We're certain our struggles are different from the struggles that brought other people to this Twelve Step program. But we listen to their stories anyway. And slowly we learn that our paths are similar. Our problems are not unique, after all.

Having hope makes every day easier, more gentle.

Having hope, we come to understand, is a decision. Other men and women have made this decision. We can too. In time we will also understand that hope makes it possible for us to expect more positive outcomes to our problems. It's so often true that what we expect is just what we get. Looking on the bright side of life can't make our struggles worse!

Having hope will open the door to my Higher Power today. Help is the by-product of hope.

Live and let live is good advice.

The more comfortable we are with the knowledge that each of us has a unique journey to make, a specific purpose to fulfill, the easier it is to let other people live their own lives. When family members are in trouble with alcohol or other drugs, it's terribly difficult to let them have their own journey. Because we love them, we feel compelled to help them get clean and sober. In reality, all we can do is pray for their safety and well-being. Their recovery is up to them and their Higher Power.

For some of us it's a leap of faith to believe there really is a Divine plan of which we are all a part. And perhaps it's not even necessary to believe. But we'll find the hours of every day gentler if we accept that a Higher Power is watching over all of us.

Being able to let others live and learn their own lessons is one of our lessons. The more we master it, the more peaceful we'll be.

I have enough to do just living my life today. I can let others do what they must.

It's so easy to get caught up in other people's lives. Assuming that we know what's best for them seems so natural. Many of us have excelled at being caretakers, but it's time to back off and let our loved ones fend for themselves. That means letting them make their own decisions and live with their own consequences.

Accepting those things we cannot change frees us.

We can't change other people. Certainly we have made others feel guilty enough so that they have given in and done things our way. And we have won many power struggles. But ultimately we can't claim ownership of anyone else's mind, and we aren't the stewards of anyone else's life. We may feel diminished by our lack of control initially, but in time we will love the freedom of living only our own lives. The extra time we'll have and the peace we'll know will comfort us.

I will experience many moments of relief and peace when I let others be their own stewards.

Impulsive reactions never benefit us.

Immediate responses to every situation aren't necessary. But sometimes we make snap decisions because we fear looking inadequate or stupid. Unfortunately, because we don't pause long enough to think through a response or to ask God for guidance, we often *do* look ignorant—just what we had hoped to avoid.

Our recovery program gives us permission to slow down, to wait for guidance from our Higher Power. It also helps us assess our strengths along with our weaknesses. Understanding that each of us is a worthwhile human being with a unique purpose is a gift of this program.

My contribution to every experience today can be according to God's will, if I ask for knowledge of it.

People grow accustomed to habits even when they are self-destructive. We who have sought the help of Al-Anon and other Twelve Step programs were often caught in patterns of behavior that injured us or other people. We want help to change these habits or we wouldn't be here now.

Changing destructive habits is what changes lives.

We learn at our first meeting that Twelve Step programs are both for the present day and for a lifetime. We are comforted and surprised by that. The comfort is in knowing help will always be available to us. The surprise is in having erroneously thought that we'd get "fixed" and not need the meetings forever.

It doesn't take us long to realize the benefits of utilizing Twelve Step recovery in our daily lives. For years we repeated the same behaviors, expecting different outcomes, but that didn't happen. Now we have a plan for living that includes Steps, slogans, friends, support meetings—a host of new options for handling every detail of our journey. And we can see, even in a short time, that our lives are changing at last.

I can change my life if I have the willingness to use what the program is teaching me.

When we have internalized Step One, our lives reflect it.

Admitting we are powerless over alcohol is not very difficult for most of us. Admitting we are <u>powerless</u> *over the alcoholic* is another matter. After all, we have used shame quite successfully to get our way on occasion. Intimidation sometimes worked. Our relentlessness sometimes wore the alcoholic down. But we never really changed that person.

Fully accepting our powerlessness over all other people may seem scary at first. (What will we do with our time?) But it makes our own lives so much simpler. Relief from worry and frustration is only the first gift. Having time to pursue our own goals comes next. Discovering happiness at will is another blessing. Once we get used to being powerless over other people, we'll realize how much living we gave up in the past.

I will find joy in my <u>powerlessness</u> today. I will have more energy for myself.

By admitting to our friends that we don't know what we should do about the many confusing, sometimes scary circumstances in our lives, we open the door for our Higher Power to reach us. That's often the way help comes to us. At times we'll open a book and an inspiring passage will jump out, or we'll wake up feeling as if God has answered us in our dreams. But more frequently and vividly, our help is in the gentle words of a friend.

Asking for help is the first step to healthy living.

Many of us postponed getting help because we dreaded asking for it. We thought that asking for help would make us look weak and uninteresting. We so wanted to be liked and admired that we pretended all was well, while in reality all was awful. It's a profound relief to share our burdens with other people. And the best part is, we'll get needed guidance.

I won't be afraid to cry "help" today. My Higher Power can help only if I'm open to it.

Hurting someone thoughtlessly just to lift our own guilt is not a proper <u>Step Nine</u>. Amends are for rebuilding the burned bridges in our lives. But if amends will hurt someone, we must decide if it's in that person's best interest to be told now. Oftentimes it's best left unsaid, but never denied to ourselves or to God.

Be careful with amends.

Changing our behavior intentionally is one part of making amends, particularly to family members who may have heard us say "I'm sorry" far too many times. Repaying money, repairing damages, and making charitable contributions on behalf of the person we have harmed are all honest attempts to right our wrong. The point in every amends attempt is to take responsibility for what we did and express our regrets. Couple this with changed behavior, and our relationships will improve immediately.

I will not shy away from any amends I need to make today, but I'll be careful not to hurt someone with information he or she doesn't need to know.

Prayer is not a requirement of Twelve Step programs like Al-Anon. In fact, the program has no requirements. It has only suggestions that if followed will change how we see our experiences. This, in turn, mysteriously changes our very experiences. One suggestion is that we seek, through prayer and meditation, to know God and God's will for us.

There is no right way to pray.

Spirituality

The idea of prayer scares some of us initially. It seems religious. However, we learn from other people, if we're open to their words, that the program is not religious but spiritual. This means that we can expect help from a Power who wants to safeguard our lives. All we have to do is let that Power in, using any method that feels comfortable. Kneeling to pray isn't for everyone. Having friendly, casual "chats" appeals to some. Others seek knowledge of God in a bird's song or a flower's blossom. Whatever is comfortable is not only adequate but appropriate.

Praying in our own special way becomes a wonderful habit. It protects us all day long, giving us strength every time we need it.

I will relish my moments with God today. They will help me in every circumstance. I'm never alone as long as I remember God.

Taking an honest look at ourselves is necessary if we want peace.

Step Four asks us to admit our character defects. That's not an easy assignment. After all, we were the ones who kept the family functioning when the chemically dependent person was making a mess of things. How "defective" could we be? In truth, we do have many assets, and it will help us to admit our defects if we also *own* our assets.

The founders of the Twelve Steps were wise men who understood the value of self-assessment. None of us is without problems, many of which we cause ourselves because of behavior we need to change. But until we can stand back from ourselves and see our part in our troubles, we'll not have the data we need to make a change in our lives. This program is designed to help us change. Its goal for us is greater peace, but we must do our part.

I will feel better today, and thus more peaceful, if I am willing to change a behavior that causes me trouble. I pray for willingness to admit my defects and own my assets.

The obsession to pressure other people to see things our way keeps us agitated. In contrast, the wisdom to understand that every person's view has validity, at least for that person, is a gift we receive from working the Twelve Steps. Our daily assignment, then, is to be patient and listen so that we may learn this lesson from women and men who have walked this path already, women and men who have come to understand that letting go of others and their addictions promises relief from the obsession that troubles each of us.

Letting go is a decision.

Look around. No one came to this particular juncture in the road because it was a hoped-for destination. Each of us ended up here because of our pain. All of us tried to force solutions that didn't fit. And we drove ourselves crazy trying to control the behavior of others, certain that "doing it our way" was not only reasonable, but right. Our past sometimes may appear to be a series of failures. But our present experience can be peaceful, hopeful, and successful. It's our decision to let go. A small decision that we can make many times today. Every day.

Let go are tiny words with huge rewards. If I want to, I can give up my attempts to control someone today. Peace will be my reward.

Only when we humbly ask for help are we ready to receive it.

On occasion, our problems seem overwhelming, and we don't know where to turn. Our job is stressful. Our health is failing. The pain of living with a drinking spouse is becoming more difficult. But many of us face no truly threatening situations, and we still have problems. Being alive, being human, means having experiences that trouble us.

It's hard to ask for help when we are in a troubling situation because we fear that means we are inadequate. After all, we are grown men and women who have taken care of ourselves and others for years. We don't have the wisdom to handle every situation, and yet we think we should. Seeking guidance from friends, sponsors, and our Higher Power gets easier with practice. Asking for help is a learned behavior. And practice we must!

But just as important as the seeking is the receiving. Are we actually open to the wisdom offered? Do we want it badly enough to truly listen to the guidance?

I will open my heart to God's wisdom today and find help for whatever troubles me.

The first of the Twelve Steps asks us to admit we are <u>powerless</u>. Our first question might be, Why? Shouldn't we try to change the conditions in our lives? Shouldn't we try to influence others to change too? If we put ourselves in good hands in this fellowship, we will begin to appreciate <u>Step One</u>. We will begin to understand that we are indeed powerless over *other* people. We can plead, complain, shame, cajole, but we cannot force them to see as we see. We will also begin to understand that we are not powerless over *ourselves*. Not today.

Nobody can change my thoughts but me.

It may seem simplistic to blame our problems on how we ourselves think. After all, others are participating in our lives too. But only we have the power to interpret the experiences we're having. And we can decide to accept every experience as an opportunity for growth and adventure, as God's will. The old-timers tell us that is what Step Three means.

I can't change anyone else; all I can change is my mind. I will carefully watch my thoughts today.

The Serenity Prayer, when relied on, changes the very nature of our lives. The reality is that most of our troubles result from an unwillingness to give up controlling the many people we encounter. What they are doing is seldom relevant. We simply want them to answer to us!

Control robs us of serenity.

There is *so* much we cannot change. Yet our stubbornness leaves us frustrated, depressed, and in near constant conflict. Nonetheless, there is an easy solution. It's the first prayer we heard in a Twelve Step meeting. We can ask God for wisdom so we can change only what is ours to change and accept all the rest. Wisdom will come. And so will the serenity we deserve.

God, grant me serenity today, along with wisdom and acceptance, so I can fulfill your will for me.

When we were young, our parents and siblings served as our teachers, but they weren't always good ones. We may have learned habits that haunt us still. Shame and guilt may still trouble us because of the messages our parents and siblings gave us. We can't undo the past teachings, but we can come to believe those teachers did their best. They passed on to us what they had been taught. Fortunately, the Twelve Step program can help us discard behaviors that serve us no more and cultivate ones that do.

Our teachers surround us.

LESSONS

We're students of life and we'll encounter many teachers. From some, we will learn patience; from others, tolerance and acceptance. A few will make us laugh. All will change us in some way. We may be apt to pass judgment on the interactions we have with others, but those with more wisdom than ourselves remind us that we can learn. In fact, we are privileged to learn something of value in absolutely every interaction. Our teachers are all around us.

I will accept that every person is my teacher today. I may be in for many surprising lessons!

Some people say there is magic in believing. Our expectations are powerful; they are self-fulfilling, in fact. And if our expectations are generally negative, we'll find the circumstances of our lives pretty dismal too.

Believing that we deserve better is the first step.

The good news is that when we expect better experiences, we'll also find them. How does this work? Surely it requires more than just believing. But it really doesn't. When we look for the good in every situation, we quite selectively see it. Making the choice to live this way means we'll regularly see opportunities for opening doors to better lives.

The formula is simple: Our Higher Power's plan for our lives is always for our benefit. Some part of that plan may be difficult to bear at first, but when we remember to believe that it is a positive opportunity, we'll feel its potential for changing our lives.

I will monitor what I believe about every experience I have today. Looking for opportunities will help me see them.

Perhaps it's human nature to grow and change only when we have to. Unrelenting pain can serve as a motivator. Sometimes ultimatums are effective too. But making excuses for others or taking over their responsibilities, even when it's for their benefit, never inspires change. Most of us came into the program because we wanted someone else to change! Now we're learning that the only change we can be certain of is one we make in ourselves.

When we do for other people what they should do for themselves, we both stay stuck.

BOUNDARIES

ENABLING T2

One of the first changes we can make is to let go of others: their opinions, their behavior, their responsibilities. Our need for them to fulfill our expectations is related to our insecurity, not theirs. Every time we preach or take on others' duties, we must recognize that we are preventing much-needed growth, ours and theirs.

Our intentions might always have been good. But the time has come to let others live their own lives. It's quite enough to take care of ourselves.

I will not do someone else's task today. Growth comes from each of us being responsible for ourselves.

T²

Our Higher Power is in charge.

TURN IT OVER

It's such a relief to give up our obsession to control, once we learn how. As we do to establish any new routine, we have to practice. In this case, we practice turning people and circumstances over to God. Our first reaction will be the familiar one, always. For so long we thought we had to be in charge. It's no wonder we felt crazy at times. We were trying to assure other people did the right thing, based on our perspective. Usually God, or they, had something else in mind.

Letting God hold the reins gives us a lot of extra time. We can narrow our focus to what we need to do today. And we can use our extra time to pray for the well-being of other people. Our payoff is feeling sane, peaceful, and rested at the end of each day.

I will enjoy the sanity of letting God take care of other people today. I'll just take care of myself.

We are learning to seek guidance on how to handle the serious circumstances of our lives. We used to feel we had to figure out everything for ourselves. What a gift it is to seek suggestions from friends we can trust. And hearing others tell how a line in a book gave them a needed answer has become a valuable tool too.

An inspiring book, a caring friend, a moment of silence—all can offer the guidance we seek.

Relying on the silence for our answers, we are less certain at first. We can't always tell if it's our ego directing us rather than our Higher Power. The important thing is that we are looking for help. We are no longer blocked by our need to be self-reliant in all matters.

Guidance is always available. We simply have to know where to look and be willing to *hear*.

I will look at my problems today as opportunities for intimacy with other people. Problems will free me from isolation.

Detachment doesn't mean denying compassion.

Approaching life with detachment may seem cold at first. We are accustomed to offering lots of help to other people. Thus the first few times we back off from what has become our natural inclination we feel uncomfortable.

Through this program we are learning so much about ourselves. For example, we never knew that we attained much of our worth from how we took care of others. Detachment doesn't mean we stop loving them. We are discovering that letting them be wholly in charge of themselves is really far more loving. And it doesn't mean we can't have deep feelings of care and concern. We simply need to stop doing for others what they need to do for themselves.

I will evaluate my need for taking care of a friend's problem today. Letting others take care of themselves is far more loving.

God's messages surround us. The twenty-four hours before us are special, never to be repeated. The people we share the day with carry our lessons within their words and actions. Let's be vigilant in our attempts to listen.

We honor the spirit in other people when we listen to them.

LEARNING T2

We have so much to learn, and that's why we're here. Our lives have purpose, even though we might fail to grasp it. Remembering that God is trying to reach us in even the most mundane of circumstances keeps us attentive to everyone in our lives. Our attention to others triggers their lessons too.

The cycle is never-ending. We are not here by accident, we are here by design. The role addiction plays in our lives is part of the design. We can learn our lessons and fulfill our purpose only by acknowledging the spirit, the presence of God, within each person God has ushered to us.

I will pay special attention to the people in my life today. It's a wonderful feeling knowing they are part of God's plan for me.

T2

Happiness is a decision.

We came into this program desperate for help and perhaps solace too. We knew our lives were more painful than most. Seeing all the smiles and hearing the laughter of the women and men at the meetings convinced us we were right! Fortunately, we have stuck around long enough to understand where their smiles and laughter are coming from.

We can experience joy regardless of whether the alcoholic is drinking or not. The example of other people has taught us this. And now *we* are the teachers for the newcomers.

The Twelve Steps are suggestions for living one day at a time. When we let the Steps guide our thinking and our actions, we discover that life doesn't have to be painful. Thinking and acting are fully in our control. Staying close to the program, even if the drinker continues to drink, can bring us happiness.

I will set a good example for someone else today. I will be living proof of the maxim "Most folks are as happy as they make up their minds to be."

Many of us assumed problems would no longer plague us once the addict got clean and sober. We're discovering that's not the case. But with a slight change in perspective, we can perceive problems as opportunities.

Sobriety is not the antidote to all problems.

Fear immobilized us in the old days. Because we weren't used to looking to a Higher Power for guidance, and because we never expected good to come from most situations, we gave up trying to make our lives better. We were resigned to tolerating life as merely a string of painful problems that we had to shoulder alone.

Very little about our lives has been the same since coming into the program. Some of us still have a drinking loved one in our lives. We may drive the same broken car or work for people who still don't appreciate us. But our lives *feel* different. We have hope where we used to have doubt. We feel love where we used to feel fear. We feel God's presence where we used to feel abandonment.

I am in good hands. No matter what is going on around me, I can feel safe and loved.

*"We admitted
we were
powerless...."*

Accepting that we cannot <u>control</u> other people's drinking is a huge step. We want what is best for them, don't we? Can't *they* see that? What we didn't understand before finding this program was that each individual is on a unique journey. What appears to us the best course to follow may not provide the lessons another person is here to learn.

And it may be dawning on us that one of *our* key lessons is how to give up trying to control someone else. Sometimes we believe we can control others because our goading or shaming gets them to give in and go along with our demands. However, we're really not in control. We are still powerless over them, and any time they want to make that clear, they will.

Accepting our <u>powerlessness</u> isn't a hopeless feeling at all, once we understand it. It offers us profound relief from the burden of responsibility for another person's life. In time this freedom will make us joyful.

Being in charge of only me *today makes my day seem so much easier.*

Our program friends are showing us how to detach from other people and their problems. We have learned we aren't the cause of a family member's alcoholism or the never-ending trauma in a friend's life, though our family and friends may try to blame us for their difficulties. The program teaches us that we don't have the power to make others go against their will. But when others cast blame our way, it's been our nature to absorb it. Now we are learning how to refuse the blame.

Other people's actions need not affect us.

Part of the problem is our desire to be liked. The anger or criticism that's directed at us hurts. Few people are wholly immune to barbs from others. Even strangers can trigger reactions in us. But we can change, we can learn detachment. Our program friends are good role models. Daily we can work at letting whatever someone else says or does roll off us. In time, detachment will become our nature.

I will ask my sponsor for help if I let someone get to me today.

*Do unto
others . . .*

RECIPROCATING
EMOTIONS

Snapping at a friend often results in being snapped at in return. That doesn't surprise us. Accusations generally elicit an angry defense and an argument. That comes as no surprise either. By contrast, being loving and compassionate toward the people in our lives generally results in others returning love and compassion to us. Why, then, is it harder to express love?

The fear of rejection is strong for many of us. Offering love while fearing it won't be returned makes us feel too vulnerable. However, the principles we are being exposed to through this program will help us understand that we do receive from others what we give. The scales are balanced. Remembering that before responding to anyone around us will make our lives far more peaceful.

I will know what to expect from others today by how I treat them. I pray to be kind and loving.

Sponsors tell us that this is a simple program we are prone to complicate. Reflecting on our lives, we probably would agree. Because we doubt that God will tell us how to handle the circumstances facing us, we aggressively move ahead, making decisions that are often not in sync with God's will and certainly not in our long-term best interests. We complicate our lives unnecessarily.

Perfection is expressing God's will enthusiastically.

Before we came into the Twelve Step program, most of us wanted to be perfect. We worked hard and oftentimes were overachievers because we needed the praises of others. Sadly, because we too often relied solely on ourselves, we missed the mark. Now we are learning to let God direct us. Each time we fulfill God's will, we'll experience the perfection and the praises we'd sought for so long. This is a much simpler way to live.

Today I will use the Third Step every time I have a question about my life.

FEBRUARY

Getting stuck in a rut of criticizing other people and ourselves is far easier than adopting a grateful attitude. But we have the choice to be grateful at this very moment. For many of us the question is *how.*

We have many things to be thankful for: We found a Twelve Step program, which has helped us see new possibilities for ourselves. We no longer hang on to self-pity for days. We ask others for guidance when we feel hopeless. We turn to a Higher Power for help in big or tiny matters, which relieves us of heavy burdens. The gratitude list goes on.

Of course we can stay stuck and ignore our blessings, but why should we? We can choose to be critical, or we can choose to feel grateful. It's up to us.

Feeling grateful is a matter of choice.

I will make a list of my blessings today. Keeping my focus on them will improve how I feel all day long.

We are empowered to decide exactly what kind of day we will have, every day.

So many times throughout the day we are inclined toward anger, frustration, criticism, or perhaps all three. We love to blame a situation or another person for how we are feeling. Many of us have shirked responsibility for our feelings and our behavior.

When we came into the program and first learned that we needed to be wholly accountable both for our feelings and for our behavior, we panicked. The responsibility seemed overwhelming. On occasion, it still does. But it's also exhilarating to know that we, and only we, can decide how we are going to feel. No one can trigger behavior that we aren't willing to display. No one can decide who we will be or how we will feel; we are the ones in charge. That's a wonderful gift.

SELF RESPONSIBILITY

I am in charge of myself today. I'll enjoy my life, all of it, if I choose to.

It's not easy to admit that we don't listen well. We may appear to be <u>listening</u> when we're deep in conversation, but how much do we really hear? There is a big difference between listening and hearing.

Listen and learn: It's a slogan that becomes more useful the more we use it.

From Twelve Step meetings and the sponsors and friends we acquire here, we have many opportunities to get the help we need, but we have to be willing first to listen and then to really hear what they tell us. <u>Learning</u> comes from hearing.

What is it that we need to hear at these meetings? We need to hear that it's possible to go on with our lives and be happy, even if the addict is still using. We need to hear that it's possible to let go of trying to control other people and live our lives only. We need to hear how others have done an inventory and have begun to look honestly at themselves instead of others for a change. And we need to hear of the relief that comes with forgiveness. Over time we'll learn many more things. This is only a beginning, but it's a good place to start.

I know others will be sharing messages I need to hear today. God, help me be willing to listen, hear, and learn.

It takes more than mere wishes to get rid of a defect.

Character defects cause our conflicts with others, trigger our self-pity, set us up for unrealistic expectations, exaggerate the "molehills," and minimize the joys. It's a fact, clear and simple, that any unhappiness is attributable to our own perception, our own response to the people and activities surrounding us. Trying to blame others for how we feel won't work once we begin working the Twelve Steps.

Accepting that we do have defects is an important phase of our recovery. It's of paramount importance that we truly believe that our defects, rather than the other people in our lives, cause our problems.

We have a responsibility to let go of our defects, replacing them with acts of love. For example, we can stop a mean-spirited remark or action, and instead we can say or do something uplifting. Quite soon we'll see that defects don't hold us hostage; our inaction does. We'll see that even a little effort reaps big changes.

I will admit to one of my defects today and consciously work to replace it with a kind act.

We don't like everyone. That's true for all of us; even the people we place on pedestals don't like everyone. But who we like or dislike matters less than our reaction to those feelings.

Let's place principles above personalities.

A Twelve Step meeting is a gathering place for men and women who are similar to the individuals we know from work or other activities. Some of them we identify with immediately. A few in the group are cynical or perhaps bossy; some are self-effacing. Some may try to manipulate the group as they used to manipulate the alcoholic or addict. In other words, the program is a "classroom" that offers us an opportunity to practice the principles we are learning.

Can we get beyond a person's actions and love him or her unconditionally, as we hope to be loved? Can we accept that we can't change a group member, except perhaps through our own good example? Can we learn to acknowledge that everyone has a perspective that has value and deserves respect? If we make progress in any of these assignments, we will enhance our relationships outside the group too. And that's what it's all about.

I don't have to like someone to show him or her the respect that every child of God deserves. The more quickly I realize this and put it into practice, the better my life will unfold.

Hopelessness exaggerates even the tiniest setbacks.

Unpleasant experiences are part of life: The traffic is snarled, or the neighbor's dog is barking again. Maybe the drinker didn't come home last night, or a friend at work seems distant. If, however, we spend our lives counting on everybody and everything living up to our expectations, we'll feel like failures and lose hope for the future.

Before discovering a Twelve Step program, many of us didn't know that we had a choice other than hopelessness. We were probably unaccustomed to relying on a spiritual program for help. Conflict or other frustrating and scary situations made us shudder. Life was arduous at best.

What a difference having hope has made. Nothing feels overwhelming for long when we remember to use the spiritual solutions found in our program.

I am given only as much as my recovery program and I can handle!

Perfection, our own and others', was (and still is, for some of us), a burdensome expectation we have dragged everywhere. And because we've expected the impossible, we've lived either in perpetual shame over our own failings or in guilt over how we have treated others who were only human.

To be human means having "defects of character."

Many of us grew up with parents who demanded perfection. We never quite satisfied them, but we did, *quite* perfectly, learn how to expect perfection from others. It's important to remember that our parents did the best they could and that we shouldn't blame them for all our defects of character. But there is something we can do about our defects.

A big load is removed from our shoulders when we give up our obsession with perfection. Although it has worked in our favor on occasion, perhaps on a work assignment, the need for perfection is not something we have always kept in perspective. Sincerely doing our best is really quite good enough. God, as we understand God, expects nothing more.

I will try to do my best today, but I will not feel ashamed if I make mistakes.

The friendships we enjoy through this Twelve Step program are unconditional, honest, intimate, and lasting.

The freedom to let people know who we *really* are is perhaps the most treasured of all the gifts of this program. For most of our lives, we suffered from the fear that if people really knew us, they wouldn't like us. Worse yet, they'd abandon us. Our perpetual fear and shame kept us isolated. And we were so alone and lonely.

Today we have friends who are as close as a quick phone call. These women and men have struggled, as we are struggling, with the power of addiction in loved ones. With our friends in the program we can openly share our fears and anger. From our friends in the program we receive solace and guidance. We feel confident that our friends accept us wholly, that they won't judge us for our actions or for the behavior of our children or spouses. We can enjoy times of peace, at last, because of these new friends.

How grateful I feel that I have friends who will be glad to hear from me if I make a call. I won't be scared and lonely today.

We believed happiness was only a dim possibility when we finally sought the help of the program. We had given up on God's fulfilling our wishes long ago. Sons and daughters were out of control. Spouses and partners were drinking and distant. Bosses were demanding and neighbors were nosy. Very few people lived up to our expectations!

We are no longer spiritually bankrupt.

GODS PLAN

A Twelve Step program was a last resort for many of us, and we weren't very hopeful. Prayers had failed us before, so why would a Higher Power be any more helpful? One of the first things we heard is that our Higher Power, or God as we understand God, answers our prayers but not necessarily on our timetable. We also learned that God gives us what we need, not what we want.

The miracle is that now we feel better than we've felt for years. For some of us, many things haven't changed: Drinkers are still drinking. Jobs are still stressful and our kids still worry us. Still, we feel hopeful, because we believe that God is taking care of us according to the plan for each of our lives. Praying for knowledge of God's will for us is a prayer that always gets answered.

I won't beseech God to do anything my way today. I'll pray to know God's way instead. My intuition can steer me.

Let's not exclude compassion for ourselves when we feel compassion.

SELF COMPASSION

It is easier to feel compassion for friends and family members who are in pain than it is to feel compassion for ourselves. But we have suffered too, or we wouldn't be in the Twelve Step program, and we wouldn't have opened this book. Pain is consistent with being human. How we handle it, how long we harbor it, how willing we are to give it up—these are ways we differ from one another.

To give up pain we first need to feel compassion for ourselves and the struggles we have had. We need to acknowledge that we have done our best. We need to be willing to care for the small child within who perhaps has always felt unworthy and inadequate. And after nurturing ourselves, we'll be more able to give up the pain that may block our growth and to help others by our example.

None of us can do it all alone. I will love myself and help my inner child handle all of life today.

What we do with our lives is not dependent on what others do with theirs. That's hard for us to believe, but we see how program friends have gone on with their dreams even though the drinker still drinks or the addict still snorts cocaine.

Our happiness doesn't depend on a loved one's sobriety.

We come into the program expecting to learn how to help our loved ones stop using. That's our primary goal. What a jolt to discover that it hasn't happened for some who share our circle. And they come to meetings anyway. More than that, they seem to be leading happy lives. At first we wonder how.

We are guaranteed happiness too. We are enmeshed with our loved ones only because we have never understood separateness. Our boundaries have been blurred. But the guidance of sponsors and the wisdom we'll gain from the meetings will show us how to disengage from others. Our first step toward the happiness we're promised is to give up our attempts to control anyone but ourselves.

I have my own dreams, my own goals. To fulfill them, I must turn my attention away from others and on to me. I can't make anyone else's life my dream.

We can't make anyone else get sober.

Most of us tried to force sobriety on our loved ones, sometimes aggressively, more often subtly. And we failed. What we learned is this: We simply can't make anyone do what that person doesn't want to do.

Learning to take responsibility *only* for ourselves is difficult when we first try. We have perhaps spent years overstepping our boundaries, doing for other people what they needed to do for themselves. And we have failed. Making other people do anything against their will is frustrating, at best.

Learning to let go, letting others do what they must, is a primary gift of this program. Coming to believe that each of us is on a unique journey, one that may not include another's sobriety according to our timetable, is a second very important gift.

I will attend to my own life today and let my loved ones take care of their lives.

Being loved unconditionally may be a new experience. Most of us were trained to get good grades or be extremely well mannered if we wanted to be loved. There were conditions, always.

We are coming to believe in unconditional love.

We may have been raised to believe in a judgmental God too. If so, the God of this fellowship seems hard to trust. ("You mean, no matter what I do, I'll be loved and forgiven by my Higher Power?")

And because of our upbringing, we may be good at setting conditions for family members and friends who want our love. For instance, we may think that they can't let us down in any way or we won't love them.

We're fortunate indeed that we have the example of so many other women and men who have walked this path before us. It has to be possible for us to change too.

We must be patient with ourselves. We lived with a very solid mind-set for many years. We won't change overnight. But we can change, if we really want to.

I will affirm that I am loved unconditionally many times throughout the day. Time will heal me and change my understanding.

Detaching
is often the
most loving
thing we
can do.

ENABLING T 2

Cleaning up the addict's messes became second nature to us. Hiding drug paraphernalia, struggling to get the addict into bed before the children woke up, calling the boss again, claiming the flu bug struck our house. Sound familiar? Because we didn't want neighbors, friends, or other family members to know what our lives were really like, we did our best to cover up the evidence.

Now we know that others probably knew the truth anyway. We were the people who denied the truth of how much alcohol was consumed, how many abuses were suffered, how many lies were told. What a relief that we are no longer resisting.

And it brings even more relief to understand that we must walk away from situations that are not ours to control, that we must leave messes to be handled by those who created them. It is not easy to detach from the turmoil others create. But from our new circle of friends in the fellowship we are learning how to do just that.

I know now that the people in my life will not learn how to take care of themselves unless I let them take care of themselves. Today is an opportunity.

Reacting to another person's craziness makes us a bit crazy too. However, someone else's anger, even if directed at us, doesn't have to trigger our anger in return.

All it takes to stop our troubling behavior is the willingness to be quiet a moment so we can think clearly before taking action. That sounds simple enough. Surely we can do it. But it takes practice, lots of it. Most of us have spent years reacting without thinking and then blaming the messy outcome on the other guy. At first, doing it the new way won't feel familiar, so our tendency will be to revert to the old behavior. Looking to the people we admire in the program for help will give us the inspiration to keep trying.

Our behavior won't be irrational if we pause and think before acting.

72

I will become adept at thinking before acting. Today will give me many opportunities to succeed.

A slogan that can help us is, Keep an open mind.

OPEN MINDEDNESS

We are so certain we are right. And part of the time we are. However, the more we grow in Al-Anon or other Twelve Step programs, the more we'll be able to let others have their own opinions. We also strive to stay flexible ourselves, in case we want to change our opinions.

We have limited knowledge today about what might happen tomorrow. God has been careful to give us only what we need to know right now. What we learn next may change the ideas we have now. Keeping an open mind allows us to be taught by God and God's teachers, all those men and women who walk among us today.

We see many experiences differently today than we'd have seen them before discovering the Twelve Step philosophy. Maybe we've fought against having an open mind, but we've changed anyway. Making the decision to "lighten up" and try on another's idea for size will affect us immensely. Our teachers can teach us only if we're willing.

I will be teachable today.

Who are we? Do we really know? If we are questioned about our strengths, do they come quickly to mind? Are we oblivious to our shortcomings, those behaviors that are at the root of many of our struggles?

Honestly accepting who we are must come first.

It's not unusual to see ourselves differently than other people do. For those of us who would rather blame others for our circumstances, acknowledging who we really are is difficult, since the next step means taking responsibility for who we are. Blaming others may let us off the hook. But it also keeps us from growing. And happiness will remain an elusive goal as long as blaming someone else appeals to us.

How do we begin to know who we really are? Fortunately, our program's founders have offered us the solution: Step Four. Doing an inventory of our behavior allows us a glimpse of who we are, at least in certain circumstances. This is a beginning. It's a process that takes time, and we're not in a race with anyone. Admitting how we have behaved and becoming willing to behave differently next time are what this program of recovery is really about.

I am who I am. But I can become the person I want to become. It's all up to me.

Believing in a Higher Power changes our perspective.

Gone are the long days of feeling adrift, days we had no hope or direction. For too long we agonized over the circumstances of our lives, tormented by the drinking and lying of our loved ones. Our attempts to control didn't work. They still won't. Yet some days we try anyway.

Most days, though, we use the principles of the program, relying on the wisdom of the first three Steps to take our focus off the person we're trying to control. Accepting that we are powerless, coming to believe in a Power that is greater than we are, letting it guide the behavior of the other person and ourselves— these things give us clarity and peace about the actions we need to take. We aren't adrift today.

I am so lucky that I have a greater Power that I can call on today. I can be certain that I'll be taken care of.

Living with active alcoholism or other drug addiction can distort our perspective. Pleading with others to quit using seldom worked and often left us hopeless and angry. Today, however, we can become more positive by regularly putting ourselves in the company of friends who have hope.

We can learn to be hopeful.

Being hopeful is an attainable attitude. Coming to believe in the presence of a Higher Power in our lives will accelerate our acceptance of hope. With the help of God and our new friends, we will firmly come to know that we are never alone, that all is well. We will experience the hope we hear in the voices of others.

I can act as if I am hopeful today, and the feelings will follow.

Accepting that we are powerless seems difficult at first.

We have felt responsible for so many people for so long that giving up our control scares us. What will *they* do? Perhaps the more important question is, what will *we* do? Where do we put our focus when we no longer put it on others?

We probably didn't understand the meaning or the value of the Serenity Prayer when we were first introduced to it. We had spent most of our lives forcing change, or at least trying to. Accepting conditions or the people we loved as they were was beyond our comprehension. After all, wouldn't they want to change if they could see themselves as we saw them?

Now we are coming to understand our powerlessness. The glimpses we get no longer scare us. Not being in charge of others anymore also means we are not to blame for their shortcomings. And that part of powerlessness we like.

I will enjoy my powerlessness today. "Giving up" the behavior of others will lighten my own load considerably.

The Big Book says that alcoholics suffer from "self-will run riot." We partners, parents, and friends of the alcoholic are afflicted with willfulness too. Our world may feel topsy-turvy every time the alcoholic is drinking and out of sight, because our own well-being has become dependent on our ability to control the drinker. The insanity is that we think we can control that person. Stress from trying to control the uncontrollable takes over our lives.

Giving up willfulness relieves the pressure.

When it is first suggested to us that we can surrender our will to God, letting God be in charge of the drinker, we are mystified and we balk. After all, how can we trust God to make the drinker do what we want?

We are slowly learning that giving up control, giving up worry, and giving up outcomes give us profound relief.

I will let the people in my life have their own lives today.

No one's behavior reflects on me but mine!

JUDGEMENT

Being embarrassed by a friend or lover's drunkenness was not uncommon. Most of us experienced that. What was also common was assuming others judged us every time the alcoholic drank.

It's difficult to give up that belief even with the input we now receive from program members. Slowly, we are beginning to understand that it is our shame that has triggered our assumptions.

Whenever we behave as respectful, well-meaning people, others can judge us only as such. If, by contrast, we choose to behave as self-centered, rude individuals, that is exactly how we will be viewed. How the alcoholic in our lives acts is not a true barometer of how others see us.

I will focus on me today and how I project myself. If I want the love and praises of others, I'll need to earn it by my actions.

Trying to solve a problem alone, without the benefit of the wisdom of other people, often leaves us stuck with an even worse problem. On the other hand, sharing any problem with interested, compassionate people, such as those we meet in the program, guarantees that many responses will surface. Each person will offer a unique and genuine perspective from which the best solution can be gleaned.

We need to share our problems to find our solutions.

It's not unusual that we kept our problems to ourselves for years. Most of us were ashamed that we didn't have perfect lives; we thought most of the people we knew did. We didn't know that our secrets kept us very stuck. Now we are learning that sharing secrets with trusted others frees us from the burden of our secrets. We can make progress toward those perfect lives only if we tell who we really are and what is really going on. What surprises have been in store for us since we joined the program!

SHAME 72

Telling a trusted friend about a problem will make this day more productive. And the problem may get solved too!

The future can be anticipated with joy.

Not being afraid of what might come tomorrow or next year is perhaps the most important of all the gifts we've received since turning our lives over to the care of God. Waiting fearfully for the other shoe to drop had become our way of life. And that might never have changed had it not been for the escalation of our pain. Some among us profess to be grateful for the pain: without it, we wouldn't have discovered this program and the peace we now enjoy.

Those of us who still live with active alcoholics or addicts could never have imagined the joy we know now. We thought they had to quit. Now we know it is we who have to quit—quit, that is, focusing on them. Consequently, we are giving our own lives the attention they have deserved for so long. We are discovering talents we didn't know we had and gaining confidence to pursue the dreams we had never before dared to dream.

Fear of the future can always return. But it's within our power to keep fear away. Using the tools we have now and relying on God to manage us can free us of fear forever.

I have nothing to fear today or any day as long as I let God take charge of me and all the circumstances in my life.

Learning to let go of the choices other people make takes away much of the angst we have grown accustomed to. Letting go of the outcome of all experiences, even those that involve us, frees our minds from the needless worry that keeps us stuck. The more we focus on a problem, our own or someone else's, the bigger it gets.

We can stop making mountains out of molehills.

Why do we worry so much? For some of us it has become a habit. Lucky for us, by sharing the Twelve Step journey we can learn how not to worry. The solution is to have faith that our Higher Power will take care of us. And the others in our lives have their Higher Power to care for them. Learning to give up our old way of "doing" life unburdens us profoundly. The time we'll gain will allow us to do what we really need to do.

My perspective today will be healthy. I'll let go and let God.

Guidance comes from many sources.

What do we think of when we hear the word *guidance?* Perhaps we recall a guidance counselor in school who told us what courses to take. Now that we are in the program we receive guidance in quite informal ways: At a meeting an old-timer will share a story that helps us make a decision. A reading in a meditation book will seem to have been written specifically for us. Or a friend will call at just the moment we are feeling fear and confusion.

Most people come into this program searching for something. We may not know just what we are missing, but we recognize a painful void. Learning that we have not only a Higher Power as a constant companion but also many new and trusted friends, we gain a fresh appreciation for guidance—what it means and how it helps. It's really everywhere, and we are learning how to tap into it, thanks to the program.

Before making any big decision today, I will listen and look for the guidance I've been assured.

Living with addiction has distorted our perception of life. We have been lied to, cheated on, and placed in danger. We've had little hope and perhaps even less confidence. It's difficult to believe that the addict isn't responsible for how we feel. But that's one of the first things we learn from our sponsor and other program members.

Our feelings are our own.

They tell us that no matter what the addict does, we are always in charge of how we feel and what we do. We can't blame other people for our reactions to the events in our lives. That's not welcome news at first. We have lived through traumatic times, and we think others deserve the blame.

It takes time to grasp the full impact of being wholly responsible for ourselves, but once we do, we begin to have hope. We are no longer defeated. We are empowered. We know no one controls us by his or her actions. The program will guide our attitude change, but we have to want it. Daily commitment will help.

No one will control me today without my consent. I can choose to be serene and hopeful about every detail of my life.

We complicate Step Six by trying to determine whether or not we are "entirely ready" to give up some character traits. Many have become strangely cherished by the time we reach the program. They have seemed like survival tactics in the midst of our personal storms. As a result, believing that we no longer need certain character traits will take willingness and courage. That's what our friends in the program can help us develop.

Defects keep us stuck.

At first it seems unlikely that we can change; after all, this is who we are. However, having friends and a Higher Power make trying to change possible. Becoming entirely ready to give up some behavioral trait comes next. As we relinquish our defective behavioral traits, one at a time, we realize how stuck we had been. And we experience genuine joy over our discovery that we can be someone different.

Today is a fresh start on being who I want to be, free of any defect.

Getting restored to sanity, as Step Two suggests, strikes many of us as odd, initially. After all, we aren't the alcoholics! We've spent years, in fact, cleaning up after the obviously insane alcoholic. Fortunately, the members of our group understand our confusion. They have been where many of us still are. And because this is a program of sharing experiences, strengths, and hopes, we'll continue learning from the "wiser" ones.

There are many degrees of insanity.

We are learning from them that the way we covered up for the alcoholic was "insane." Our obsession with what they were doing, where they were, and whether they were using or not was also insanity. Most of all, thinking that we could control them by our pleas, our anger, and our silence was as insane as much of their behavior.

What a relief it is to be giving up our obsession. Sanity is attainable, at least for us. Our friends and our Higher Power are here to help.

I know the difference between sane and insane behavior. With God's help, I'll behave sanely today.

MARCH

At first, we may be confused about how to nurture the "inner child." Fortunately, we can learn from other people in the program that to nurture our inner child, we need to give it our attention, comfort, and support.

Loving our inner child is a first step to health and wholeness.

The inner child is the lonely part of us that feels fear first. Our adult self can be taught to reach out to and walk with that child along the dark passageways. We can protect that child from the cruel barbs of others. Visualizing our arms cradling that small child will initiate the genuine love for ourselves that's been lacking. The bond created fills a void that has haunted us.

After we have connected with our inner child, we will find it easier to connect with the people we care about. The sadness we all share as members of the human community is lack of enough love—for ourselves and others. Through the program we are learning to be catalysts for love.

I will meditate on my inner child's needs today. I will be loving and attentive toward not only my inner child but also other people.

Sponsors keep the program alive.

The founders of Alcoholics Anonymous understood the importance of telling other people how they had overcome the struggles and multiplied the successes in their lives. Sponsorship is a key element in every Twelve Step program. Every one of us reading these words has a part to play.

Sharing our experiences with newcomers or old-timers is equally valuable. None of us has the perfect program. We are always learning and relearning to use the tools that promise saner living. Every time we answer a call for help or offer ourselves as a sounding board to a friend in pain, we'll have an opportunity to strengthen our program.

The program continues to thrive because individuals keep talking to each other and seeking from one another the wisdom that can make each new day more serene.

I will have an opportunity to help someone today. God sees to that every day. I pray for the willingness to do my part.

The Third Step suggests that we turn our will over to God. That's a stumbling block for many of us. We don't know how to do it, and it's not easy for our friends in the program to explain the process. With patience, though, we come to realize it's more a feeling than anything else.

We can know the difference between God's will and our will.

Pushing our will on someone else results in conflict and tension. We can learn to recognize negative feelings as signs that we're not doing God's will. Becoming willing to pause long enough to ask ourselves what God would want us to do in a specific situation, and then doing it, assures us that God's will, not our will, is in charge. We'll then feel peace.

Recovery is showing us the difference between peace and tension, God's will and our will. Willingness to try a better way to live with others guarantees that we'll recognize God's will every moment, if that's our desire.

I want to feel peaceful today. Asking for knowledge of God's will and then following it will make me peaceful.

Believing in the possibility of change gives us hope.

For a long time, with little or no success, we have struggled to make others do as we wish. We can't control people, no matter how sophisticated our manipulations are. If they want to drink, they do. If they want to lie, they do. We just can't stop them!

With the help of our friends in this program, we are learning a better way to live. We hear laughter in their voices. We see serenity in their faces. We know from their stories how similar our struggles have been. But they are free from despair. And we can be too.

We can change. We are changing. Believing in change makes it possible.

My affirmation today is "I can be as hopeful and happy as I decide to be."

Coming to believe that we are not responsible for solving anyone else's problems or making anyone else's decisions frees us to pursue our own dreams and aspirations with greater concentration. But it's not easy to give up our control of other people. It's how we thought we were supposed to live. Their burdens had become ours.

Accepting powerlessness lightens our burdens.

We surely have lots more time to take care of ourselves now that we have begun letting others be in charge of themselves. But we have to watch out for slipping back into our old controlling behaviors. Ingrained habits are hard to change. We have to learn how to savor the extra hours in our day now that we only have ourselves to control. As our accomplishments multiply, we'll find that letting others take care of themselves will be easier.

I am in charge of myself. What do I want to accomplish? I can begin right away.

We can stop creating conflict where none need exist.

Human interactions often result in conflict. If we can't accept someone else's opinion or decision, conflict will occur. But we can develop the ability to accept how other people view the world. Using the Serenity Prayer regularly is a good beginning.

Alcoholism is a disease that affects the entire family. One of the signs we exhibit as family members of the alcoholic is control. We try to control others' drinking, emotions, opinions, and behavior. We may try to control outcomes to situations that don't even affect us. Learning to let go of others' opinions and actions is possible. We can come to believe that every human being's journey is unique. We can even learn to accept the idea that our separate journeys and realities are what enrich our lives.

I will honor everyone's way of living today. Practicing this one day at a time will become a healthy habit.

When in the midst of turmoil, we resist quietly praying and trusting God to resolve the
problem. We want to do something on our
own. We want to change the circumstances
that are troubling us. Praying doesn't seem
enough: It's just too passive .

*Prayer eases
our minds.*

Prayer isn't new to most of us. Before
coming into a Twelve Step program, we had
prayed all the time for the alcoholic: "Please,
God, make him stop drinking." "Please, God,
get her home safely." "Please, God, don't let
them embarrass the family." What's different
now is that we are learning to pray "for
knowledge of [God's] will for us," instead of
asking God to change other people to our
specifications.

From our friends and sponsors, we are
learning that at the right time, in the right
way, God will change what needs changing in
others' lives. Prayer is still very helpful. In particular, it quiets our minds. But God's
timetable is out of our hands.

*It's natural to want to know God's will for
everyone, but I'll be grateful to know it just for
myself. In the quiet of my mind, I'll know.*

Turning the other cheek doesn't mean giving up our right to respond.

ASSERTIVENESS

Revenge is not an option once we get accustomed to the Twelve Step principles. It never did give us more than a short-term rush, and it usually left us with guilt—lots of it. Now we are learning to acknowledge the boundaries between us and other people. This helps us detach from their mean-spiritedness, which often has prompted our own vengeful behavior.

It's important to distinguish between letting others stomp on us and letting them have their behavior. The program doesn't say we should take abuse; it suggests instead that we rationally tailor our response, relying on God as our speechwriter. If we respond calmly and firmly, without attacking, we give all concerned an opportunity to calm down.

Far fewer will be the times we're haunted by guilt if we follow this action plan. Acting responsibly, with God's help, will feel right and honorable to ourselves and the "opposition."

I need to stand up for myself always and, just as important, rely on God for support.

The <u>Serenity Prayer</u> has the potential of changing our lives concretely. The hardest part is remembering to rely on it. What the prayer offers is an opportunity to quiet our minds long enough to sense what our Higher Power wishes for us. In the stillness, we'll find the courage to accept what we must and the strength to change what we need to change.

"God, grant me the serenity . . ."

It's not unusual to think that everyone but us needs to change. Ask around at meetings. All will agree that we came to our first meeting thinking we'd learn how to get other people to change, certain that would make us happy. But that's not how happiness comes, and we're lucky for that. If our happiness were tied to what others did, we'd always be in their control. What a bleak existence that might be!

The happiness we deserve will come when we do two things: first, take the power that is ours through becoming willing to accept others as they are; and second, make a commitment to change what we need to change and then follow through. Using the Serenity Prayer puts us in charge of our own happiness.

I will find as much happiness as I want today. The Serenity Prayer, used often, will be the key.

We can't get away with ~~blaming~~ other people anymore.

ARGUING

EXPECTATIONS

Daily we are in situations that can erupt in conflict. How we handle ourselves, particularly our thoughts, contributes to the conflict's escalation or defusion. Fortunately, we have the ability to control our thoughts. There aren't many areas of our lives about which we can be so confident.

The impact our thoughts have on us—and others too—is awesome. What we think about the people we'll meet today influences how we'll treat them. That, in turn, contributes to how they treat us. How we perceive our own strengths and opportunities controls the way we pursue our careers and our goals. The expectations we cultivate of ourselves and others tend to become true, as long as we don't expect perfection.

I want to take responsibility for my thoughts. Blaming others became an easy habit, but it never did me any favors. I will be careful about what my mind cultivates today.

Living with an alcoholic partner or parenting an addicted child without support from other people who understood nearly destroyed many of us. How we finally found the help we now have may still baffle us. But we did find help, and it wasn't an accident. Our willingness to surrender our isolation, our shame, our belief that we could "do it alone," made it possible to accept help.

The support we now count on from others and from God will always be available. Shouldering any problem alone, grave or small, is never necessary. And providing support to others who are also in pain, giving back some of what we have been given, nourishes the active flow of help.

We have support from friends, the principles of this program, and a Higher Power.

I am in a circle of support. What I give to others will return to me. No problem will be too heavy for any of us today.

Hopelessness haunts us no more.

Hopelessness often threatens to darken our perspective. It may take months, even years, in this fellowship to fully believe that we have a Higher Power who wants to help us every moment. But it's true.

We can look forward to a serene outlook on every encounter today if we remember that God will be along for the ride. So much of what was expected of us in years past filled us with dread because we thought we were alone. We feared we couldn't cope with our situations. Now we have hope, serenity, and faith that all is well, and all will always be well, because our Higher Power is as close as our breath.

With every breath today I will try and remember that God is part of me, now and forever.

Many of us are trying to live "normal" lives, even though someone we love is still actively addicted. It's seldom easy to go to work, handle household chores, and give loving attention to the many people in our daily lives when we are consumed with worry about the still-struggling user.

Accepting other people as they are will give us peace.

Coming to believe that all people have a Higher Power watching over them gives us some relief from the worry that haunts us. We cannot change others. We cannot make a spouse, partner, friend, or child choose the sober life. We cannot control any action that another person takes. But we can accept other people as they are and decide to take control of our own thinking and actions.

Learning to accept our loved ones as they are will empower us to begin accepting other people as they are too. What a gift!

I will practice acceptance every time I feel agitated with someone today. I know acceptance can become a healthy habit with enough practice.

T²

Step Six asks us to become entirely ready to let God have our defects. What does that mean? None of us wants troublesome defects. And yet some of them served as survival skills in the past; thus today we may fear parting with them. Listening to sponsors and other program winners helps us see that every defect, in time, turns on us. While it might have helped us cope at one time, it now is killing our spirit, our hope, our relationships.

Strengthening assets minimizes defects.

CHARACTER ASSETS

It's not easy to give up a defect to God. The void this leaves needs filling. Fortunately, sponsors and other people suggest how to fill the void. And that's where our assets come in. No matter how low our self-worth, regardless of how inadequate we feel, we all have special positive qualities too. We can take any one of them and demonstrate it in our lives, every day, or even many times a day. We'll feel empowered, hopeful, and far less encumbered by the traits that have caused us so much pain.

I will focus on my assets today, and I'll let others see them at work too.

What does our Higher Power have in store for us today? Although we can't anticipate exactly what will happen, we can be sure that it will be for our education and our benefit.

Hindsight makes it easy to see how the painful situations changed us and helped us grow. But it's easy to overlook the mundane, everyday experiences that contribute to who we are becoming. These experiences strengthen our willingness to be patient with and accepting of others. The quiet experiences of daily life can teach us to set aside intolerance and judgment of others. Learning to love will have a positive impact on every aspect of our lives.

Even ordinary experiences have much to teach us.

LESSONS

Within the ordinary experiences I will find my teachers today. I will be observant.

Asking God for help is a sign of strength, not of weakness.

Before joining the program we didn't think we could ask anyone else for help. We mistakenly thought it was a sign of weakness and we had to be strong. How scared we were on occasion, and yet how unwilling we were to ask for help. T²

Coming to the program was our first step in breaking through the barrier. Since then, our willingness to continue asking for help has given us hope and growth we would never have attained otherwise.

Step Seven suggests that we ask God for the help we need. For some of us, it's easier to ask God for help than a human being. But the real lesson here is simply *the asking.* Admitting that we need help, that we can't do anything alone, makes us aware of our connection to all of life. That makes us peaceful. We feel secure. We belong. We are like others: We need them, and they us.

I will know that all is well today if I turn to God for whatever help I need. I don't need to do anything all alone.

Resenting other people is common. We resent the glory that people we don't like achieve. We resent the success of neighbors if we're experiencing little of it in our own lives. We resent the good looks and the good luck that certain friends enjoy. And we certainly resent the practicing addicts among us when we are working so hard to change them!

How can we give up resentment when we feel it so naturally? It never seems that we decide to feel it; we just do. But from the men and women in this program we are learning that we do make a decision to be resentful each time we are, and it never makes us feel good. In fact, our spirits are burdened every time we harbor resentment.

Sponsors tell us to pray for those we resent, pray that they too will receive all the blessings we hope to receive in our lives. That seems impossible before we try it. But once we do, we feel miraculously uplifted.

Some short-comings seem to hang on.

I am hanging on to some shortcomings. Today I'll ask myself why and make a conscious decision to ask God to help me let go of them, just for today.

Keeping life simple and quiet may at first seem boring. Many of us were used to living in extremes: Situations were either going our way and we were ecstatic, or all hell had broken loose and we were enraged, perhaps even suicidal. It was our perspective, often a faulty one, that defined the way situations appeared. Creating chaos had become normal.

Living on the edge has lost its appeal.

Our new life in recovery may at first seem strange. But in time deciding we want to live serenely and slowing down so we can think through circumstances before responding will begin to feel normal. How fortunate that we have a blueprint for doing this. The Twelve Steps and the slogans will make possible whatever change we want to make.

I didn't know what serenity was before coming to a Twelve Step program. But it's mine today and every day if I want it.

It's not unusual to feel we don't fit in. As youngsters we might have been self-conscious, and growing up doesn't necessarily change that. We want to be like other people; we think that will relieve our anxiety, remove our loneliness. Consequently, we adopt values that aren't comfortable and behaviors that are foreign. But the pain remains.

Respecting our individuality is part of recovery.

Pain from many sources brought us to the program. One of the first things we discovered is how like these people we were. What a joy! But there's a danger in that too. It can prevent us from acknowledging our special differences.

Feeling that we belong, that we fit in, doesn't mean that we are like others in every way. That would rob us of the qualities necessary for making our individual contribution to God's big picture. Appreciating our differences rather than being afraid of them will come in time. For now, we can trust the process of change.

I do fit into God's plan for the universe. My qualities are unique and needed for the unfolding of the whole picture.

Willfulness and serenity cannot coexist.

Every day we encounter people who exude peacefulness. We wonder how they attained it. If we watch them closely, we'll notice how accepting they are of people. They seem not to be bothered by conflicting opinions, unconcerned with decisions that don't affect them, uninterested in controlling circumstances that involve others. They are far different from us.

Why are we so willful? It nearly always causes tension, yet we say we want peace. Letting others travel their own paths rather than trying to force them to travel ours is no reflection on how much we care, but do we really believe this? Perhaps not, and so we exert our will.

Living with someone who struggles in the throes of addiction gives us far too many opportunities every day to try willfulness. The decision to try peacefulness instead will change how this day measures up.

I can give my will to God today. Every time I open my mouth to correct or control someone else, I'll stop and ask God to take over for me.

All of us reading these pages and sharing these meetings have made a profound decision: We have become willing to ask other people for help. We have quit living in isolation with our problems. Most of us feared letting others know what our lives were really like. How refreshing to learn that our struggles and shame are manageable, that others have lived through equally trying experiences, some perhaps even worse than our own.

Seeking help or staying isolated— it's a decision we make every day.

Support

Living in isolation for so long made it hard to trust our new friends right away. But patience, coupled with listening to their stories, has taught us that it's safe to reveal our secrets. We all have them. We all gain from one another's vulnerability.

Deciding to get help and reflecting on the good that has come from that decision make it easier to take action on other matters. Twelve Step meetings and sponsors give us ready sounding boards whenever we need clarity and guidance. We'll live in isolation no more.

Today I'll not stew in isolation. I will ask for help when I need it.

Hearing how others have handled experiences similar to ours makes us aware that our old behaviors didn't serve us very well. We also learn that any situation can be handled with the support of the Twelve Step fellowship.

In time we also come to appreciate what we gain by sharing with newcomers how we have survived painful, humiliating experiences. This gives them hope and a pattern to follow, similar to the one we received from the old-timers. We are also reminded of our strength to handle truly difficult experiences. We aren't guaranteed a reprieve from them just because we are in a Twelve Step program. Thus we need the reminder occasionally as an antidote to troubled times.

We benefit by sharing our experience, strength, and hope.

If a friend is troubled today, I will tap my own memory and offer what I have learned. Recalling my own troubled times will give me a measure of my growth.

We have all suffered humiliation. Perhaps a spouse ridiculed us in public or a parent's disorderly conduct shamed us in front of our friends. Perhaps a boss criticized us in front of co-workers.

Being humiliated is not the same as having humility.

However, we could have refused to let our egos be injured. Had we then the tools we have now, we could have felt compassion for the perpetrator. No healthy person heaps injury of any kind on another struggling soul. The program taught us this.

We have learned about true humility. To be humble is to surrender, to give up trying to change people or circumstances, to give up trying to force our will upon others. Humility is being quiet, being at rest, and being confident that God is present in every situation. Humility is being at peace, always.

No one can humiliate me today unless I accept that condition.

It's only moment by moment that we experience life.

Worrying distorts our perception of an experience. It takes away the spontaneous joy that we might have known. Even more troubling, it compromises our ability to be present in the moment. When we worry, we aren't in touch with what is happening in the present. Meanwhile, our lives can pass us by.

There are so many things we can learn from Al-Anon or other Twelve Step programs. We can learn to live in the here and now. We can adopt a new set of values if the ones we've been living by serve us no more. We can learn from the experiences of others how to save ourselves from unnecessary pain. We can get to know our assets and our defects. And we can learn to rebuild bridges to link ourselves with other people, bridges that were burned in the past.

Changing our lives with the help of the program gives us hope that we can begin to experience God's plan for us as it unfolds moment by moment. Nothing can bring us greater freedom.

I can live in the present moment. With determination I can let my worries go.

Our first introduction to Step Three scares many of us. "You mean I can't do what I want anymore, that I'm no longer in charge of me?" we ask. What we come to understand from the shared wisdom of other people is that a caring God, however we define God, will give us comfort, direction, and the sense that we are no longer *ever* alone. And once we have grown used to relying on our Higher Power for help, we won't want to go back to how we lived before.

Making a decision to let God give us guidance eases our burdens.

How many years did we struggle to make the right decision? Oftentimes our decisions affected more people than just ourselves. We fretted over the long-term effects. But no longer do we need to lose sleep over any situation. Our reliance on the guidance we have been promised will take the worry out of our lives, giving us time to accomplish goals that have been long forgotten.

I feel as if I've been given a new lease on life. What a good landlord my Higher Power is.

Feeling equal to other people is a learned behavior.

We compare ourselves to others so automatically that we're seldom conscious of it. It's how we measure our worth. Feeling superior or inferior to others might be how we were raised to see the world, but there is another way. From the program we are learning that it's possible to recognize everyone's worth, to honor the equality of us all.

Practicing this new perception until it becomes automatic will have a profound impact on every circumstance in our lives. When we feel equal to others, they will no longer intimidate us and we will no longer try to shame them. Conflict will subside. Anxiety will recede. When we acknowledge them and ourselves as valuable, necessary, equal, contributing members of society, we will discover a world far different from the one we have known. And we will feel a peace, a joy, that visited us but rarely.

If I want to be at peace today, I need to remember that I am equal to everyone else.

As children, most of us were introduced to God. No doubt we learned a few prayers and recited them at specified times. But as adults, we have been much more accustomed to trying to handle problems by ourselves. We thought admitting our fears to others made us look weak and gave them power over us, and asking God for help was a coward's way out. Thus our adult lives have been fraught with anxious moments.

Fear opens the door to our Higher Power.

Now we see that those of us who have relied on God have handled our fears more successfully than those of us who've gone it alone. Finally, we are coming to believe it's never too late to change our perception of God's role. Making the decision "to turn our will and our lives over to the care of God" keeps the door to God open and the fear at bay.

When I feel fear today I'll turn to God for the help I've been promised. And then I'll take Step Three.

We can handle everything as it is, just for today.

We want to change so many aspects of our lives. We want drinkers to get sober, jobs to be more fulfilling, defects to disappear. And we want it all to happen today! Impatience complicates the flow of our lives. "We get what we need when we need it," say the wiser ones among us. Little by little we are coming to believe that there is a timetable for how our lives unfold; it simply is God's timetable, not ours.

What helps us accept this is believing that we can handle everything as it is, just for today. Surely one more day of a job we don't like can be tolerated. Living with an active addict can be handled too if we keep our focus on today only. Some new, positive behavior such as regularly saying more than just a cursory hello to other people can be tried just for today. The results will astound us. The possibilities will excite us.

Living just for today will give us a fresh outlook on every day as it unfolds. Few things will overwhelm us when we keep our focus on today.

I look forward to every experience today, knowing that God is giving me what I need.

Any skill we are trying to develop takes practice. We learn to cook, use a computer, play a sport, or fly a plane only after lots of hours of dedicated attention. We may want to be good at what we do immediately, but we don't really expect it. It's much the same with the Twelve Steps. Daily application of them will improve our lives. But we can't simply *wish* our lives would change.

Twelve Step principles, if given daily attention, will change our lives.

PRACTICING THE PRINCIPLES

SUPPORT

It's wonderful to realize that we do have a process for changing how we feel each day. Now the small thrills can come at will, simply when we use one of the Steps to handle whatever we are feeling or thinking. The only thing we will have spent is the time it took to remember to use the program. With practice, using the Twelve Step principles will become second nature.

My day will be manageable when I remember to use the Steps.

Becoming quiet brings the search for answers to an end.

MEDITATION

Problems are opportunities for growth. They let us experience the wisdom of other people when we ask for help. They assure us a better connection to our Higher Power if we want it. And they give us chances to practice inner silence and find the place where all answers ultimately reside. Going within offers us profound calm, the love and the secure comfort of our Higher Power. Until we have sampled that gift, we can't fathom what we have missed in life. Acknowledging the presence of God changes every situation we encounter. It changes every detail of every day.

Let's not fear problems. Instead, let's see them as mere reminders that we have forgotten to remember the presence of our Higher Power. Taking a few moments to travel within will bring us clarity and comfort. Peace will come along with the problem's resolution.

I will receive the answer I need if I look in the right place.

Some of us may have arrogance as one of our character defects. However, more of us probably have a poor self-image. In fact, it's fairly common to think that we're worse than most of our peers. It seems we feel one extreme or the other.

Humility is a gift of the Fifth Step.

Revealing to another human being and to God all the elements of our behavior will help us realize how typical we are. It's humbling, perhaps surprising, and always comforting to learn how much like other people we really are. Our Fifth Step listener will guide this understanding.

EQUALITY

Accepting ourselves as equal to others is unfamiliar territory. But taking this step will help us grow, and we'll appreciate its value as we continue our commitment to doing the necessary footwork.

I am who I am, much like all the other people around me. And that's good. I'll appreciate it today.

APRIL

The first prayer we hear in most meetings is the Serenity Prayer. It's a simple, beautiful prayer, and we repeat it without grasping its meaning. Accepting what we can't change at first mystifies us; changing what we can pushes our limits of understanding; having "the wisdom to know the difference" is beyond us. So how will we learn about wisdom? It's best to watch those we look up to in our meetings.

How hard is it to acquire wisdom?

They will show us how they keep their attention on themselves and their own behavior. They don't complain about spouses or kids or friends. Instead, they talk about their struggles with their own behavior, and they emphasize how a Step gives them assistance and hope. We observe that they rely on prayer and, even more important, meditation, for their answers.

We see how quietly they go about their lives. They carry stillness with them, it seems, and they exude strength. Both must come from their dependence on a Higher Power. They tell us they adhere to the principles of the program in all matters. And we realize that although acquiring wisdom is not beyond us, it will take effort and willingness and commitment.

If I want to acquire the wisdom to live serenely, I must be willing to do the work the program suggests. I will begin today.

Nobody has all the answers— nobody, that is, except our Higher Power.

GUIDANCE

We are suffering from the illness of alcoholism, even though we aren't alcoholics. A "symptom" is that we think we know what's best for everybody. Whether or not we are asked for advice, we often feel compelled to give it. Our life's work has been to control as much of other people's lives as we can get away with.

Thank God that in the Twelve Step program we are beginning to learn that others must be in charge of themselves. They must plan their own lives. They must solve their own problems. And the *help* they need to rely on comes from their Higher Power, not from us.

We will know greater joy and peace when we, too, rely on our Higher Power for the solutions to our problems. Alone, we don't have all the answers. We don't need to. We will be told what we need to know if we ask for the guidance we've been promised. The program is helping us. It's helping our loved ones too.

I will acknowledge that I need my Higher Power for my answers today. I'll suggest my friends look to their Higher Power for their answers too.

We generally expect to find words of wisdom in great literature, so we look for them there. And when we listen to learned scholars, we assume their words are tempered with wisdom; thus we listen closely. At meetings we hear many words of wisdom, and oftentimes they are uttered by the newest member of the group when we least expect it.

What we are learning is that the answers we seek are always within our grasp if we open ourselves to the information that surrounds us. The program books we've been introduced to, the sponsors who offer suggestions, and the speakers at the weekly meetings all have wise words for us. Our effort to listen will reward us richly. The wise guidance we seek will come to us.

If we listen closely, we'll hear wisdom from the most unexpected sources.

I will be alert to the utterances of everyone today. I can't assume I know who will offer the wisdom I seek.

I help my sponsor when I ask for help.

STEP TWELVE

When we first hear that sponsors are helped even more than sponsees when help is sought, we don't believe it. Sponsors run good programs, or we wouldn't have asked them to sponsor us. What we don't understand until that time when someone seeks us out is that our program stays fresh only if we give it away to other people. This means that the more we share our own experiences, strengths, and hopes, the healthier we become.

Our growth is up to us. We will continue getting healthier and happier as long as we stay committed to sharing the program message. But we will have occasional "slips," times when we fail to use the tools we thought we had mastered. Sponsorship comes in very handy then. Telling a sponsee what has worked for us helps us see how we have let the tool slip from our hands and allows us to rediscover it for ourselves.

The circle of help—from sponsor to sponsee to sponsor again—assures the continued well-being of us all. None of us can maintain a healthy life in isolation.

Knowing I may help my sponsor if I ask for help today makes it easier to ask. I will be willing to fulfill my part of the circle.

At first it is difficult to believe that we can be happy, even though our loved ones continue drinking, using other drugs, or both. Our happiness has been on hold. It has been tied to their abstinence; thus it has always been a hoped-for future experience.

We are coming to believe. . . .

FAITH

What a shock to discover that we can be happy anyway! All around us at every meeting are women and men who live daily with active alcoholism and addiction. We hear their laughter. We see the hope on their faces. We hear their stories of triumph. And we know we are witnessing genuine happiness. Their examples give us the courage we need. And in time we too will give others courage by our example. Each of us is strengthened by the presence and example of one another.

Knowing other people have traveled my path and found happiness gives me courage and hope. They are my teachers; I am their student.

We are not responsible for someone else's journey.

We have assumed responsibility for or made excuses for other people's actions throughout much of our lives. Maybe we did children's overdue homework or called in sick for a hungover spouse. As children, we may have pretended a passed-out parent was ill or away rather than admit the truth. We were far too concerned that others' behavior somehow reflected on who we were. Being responsible for much more than just ourselves came easy.

Now, learning to let others be responsible for themselves troubles us sometimes. It feels as if we are letting them down. In reality, we are letting them grow up. From this fellowship we are learning that for everyone there is a path, for everyone there is a purpose. We must let others make their own journeys in order that we may stay focused on our journey.

I sometimes still want to take responsibility for someone else. However, wanting to and actually doing it are two different things.

We may be skeptical of ever finding joy or security. What a blessing, then, to hear from our fellowship friends that we have the power to feel gratitude for what we have learned, even from the most painful experiences. We can change our feelings toward many of our difficult experiences if we change our perspective.

We can be grateful for every experience if we change our attitude.

We have all heard the adage, *If life gives you lemons, make lemonade.* But do we feel the profundity of that saying? What we do with our experiences is up to us. A drinking partner can be tolerated if we focus on acceptance and patience. An irate co-worker can be forgiven when we remember our Higher Power gives us no more than we can handle. Our attitude, in fact, can save us or break us in every instance. Gratitude is nothing more than a decision to look at problems with a fresh perspective.

My mind awaits whatever I decide to put in it. I control the kind of day I will have.

*Alcoholics
suffer from
"self-will
run riot."
We do too!*

Being certain that we were right, that our way was the right way, was part of our old lives. Many of us fell into the habit of picking up the pieces when a spouse or other family member made a mess of some situation. And that fueled our belief that we knew best.

In regard to some circumstances, we probably do know best. After all, each of us is right some of the time. But learning to back off from a situation, even when it appears we are right, empowers us. Not *having* to be right gives us a new freedom. It lessens the tension between us and other people. It relieves us of the burden of trying to make outcomes match our expectations.

Our path through life will be easier to navigate if we try to be right only regarding ourselves.

Today I will only decide what's right for me.

The disease of alcoholism has affected us too. One of the signs is wanting every circumstance that touches us to be handled our way, right now! What often happens is that we take over the responsibilities of someone else. Conflict arises, a power struggle ensues, and a relationship is once again strained.

To let go means to stop.

There are moments when we can't imagine letting go of an outcome, at least not when we will be affected. It's fortunate that other people testify to how well their lives are going since they have dared to let go, because that gives us courage to do the same. When we finally do let go, we realize first how free we feel. Second, we are peaceful. Third, the tension, so common to our relationships, is gone.

To let go means to stop: stop talking, stop arguing, stop manipulating, stop whining, stop fantasizing about what should be, stop every action that is meant to control or change someone else. The result will be transformed lives, ours and those close to us.

I will stop whatever I'm about to do today and think it through. If I'm intent on changing someone else, I'll stop myself.

Crises are facts of life.

No doubt we thought we'd be free from crisis after seeking help in this program. Having a crisis now, however, may shake us up even more than in the past. While these Twelve Steps will change our lives dramatically, they won't prevent difficult circumstances from occurring. The journeys of the many travelers we encounter in life can lead to conflict. And conflicts can become crises.

That's why we are learning new behaviors for interacting with others, behaviors that will help us avoid exaggerating the elements of a conflict. Our ability to do this comes with practice and the willingness to let others have their own opinions. We are also learning that letting a Higher Power take charge of our lives takes us out of the driver's seat. Many a crash is thwarted when we quit steering.

I don't have to push a conflict to a crisis today. Instead, I can put my focus on God.

Before calling it a day let's look honestly at who we were today. Were we thoughtful and courteous to our friends and lovers? Did we criticize them for not living up to our expectations? Did we put ourselves down for not measuring up to the standards of someone else? Did we ask our Higher Power for guidance, or were we ego-bound?

Taking an inventory helps us know who we really are.

Getting to know who we are is crucial if we are to change. Doing a daily inventory reflects our willingness to look at ourselves. Most of us want to make changes, or we wouldn't be here in this program. However, we don't have to change everything at once. In fact, that wouldn't be possible. Let's just focus on a small change. Evaluating ourselves at the end of each day will clarify what we need to do differently.

I can be the person I really want to be if I know which behaviors I need to change. I'll do an inventory today.

The present moment is all we are certain of.

LIVING IN THE MOMENT

How we lament the past! Why didn't we handle that situation differently? *If only* we had not given in! We like to think that if we could replay the past, we could do it more successfully, certainly less painfully. But the past is gone. We lived it as honestly and thoughtfully as we knew how at the time.

Anticipating the future seduces us as well. "What will I say if he doesn't come home?" "Should I apologize if she seems mad?" "Will my boss expect me to handle something I am unfamiliar with?" Using the hours we waste worrying about future possibilities, we could finish many of today's projects. And reflection on our lives shows us that most of the things we worried about didn't happen anyway.

Right now, this moment is the only one we can be certain of. Of course, we can also be certain that we have a Higher Power to help us handle whatever emerges in every moment of today.

I will live today moment by moment. I will be prepared for the future when it comes.

Today will be what we make it. Regardless of the weather, the kinds of work to be done, the personalities crossing our paths, we'll feel joy and peace if that is our choice.

Attitude is everything!

Agonizing over circumstances that aren't to our liking or dwelling on our failure to control other people, whether friends or foes, has robbed us of the happiness that is always ours to experience. Depression, anger, fear, and frustration shadowed our steps because we didn't take control of the only thing that's ever been in our control absolutely—attitude.

It's so easy to blame others for every wrinkle in our lives. But as we grow accustomed to the idea of taking full responsibility for how we think and feel, we'll be empowered. No longer will our sense of self feel diminished. And, as Abraham Lincoln is credited with saying, we will be just as happy as we make up our minds to be.

Nobody can mess with my attitude but me!

*A crisis
is an
opportunity
to rely on
our Higher
Power.*

When we came to this program, we were told
right away that a Higher Power is watching
out for us and that we can look to that Power
whenever we want guidance or peacefulness.
Let's not resist this invitation.

Most of us had daily crises before turning
to this program for help. Our attempts to
control other people caused many of these
crises. So did our reactions to the natural ebb
and flow of human existence. Now we have
to take the plunge and begin to rely on our
God, however we understand God, to show
us the way to handle every experience that's
part of our Divine unfolding.

GUIDANCE TO
FROM GOD

*I will look to God today, and every experience
will make sense in the whole of my existence.*

Despair was a familiar home to many of us. We thought it was our fault that our loved ones drank too much. If only we could control our reactions to situations, they wouldn't drink, we told ourselves. Maybe. Repeatedly we tried to talk them out of that next drink. And just as often, we failed. What am I doing wrong? we wondered.

Many of us came to this program spiritually bankrupt.

Today we can feel grateful for the hopelessness that haunted us. It brought us to this program that is giving us back our lives. At last we can make thoughtful decisions beneficial to our well-being. We can handle problems, large or small, with the certainty that we'll survive them. We are learning, daily, the boundary between the situations that are ours to control and the situations that clearly belong to someone else. Most importantly, we know we are never alone. Not only do we have the company of other people who have made a similar journey, but we have a Higher Power. We understand, now, that we were never alone. We simply failed to feel *the presence*.

The greatest gift I have been given is the knowledge that God will help me make every decision I face today.

Listening is a wonderful gift we can choose to open each day.

Intently listening to each person who crosses our path is a most difficult assignment. But only by listening do we gather our daily lessons and significant messages from our Higher Power. When it's hard to listen because we don't like what someone is saying, we have to consider why. Evaluating our own perceptions and letting go of others' opinions are important lessons.

We all play key roles in each other's lives. It's not coincidental that we share this path at this time. The people we meet, work with, live with—all are necessary to our Divine journey. From this program we are gathering the tools that will ease the steps of our journey. Listening is a significant tool. Let's be glad for every opportunity to strengthen our listening skills.

My mind may wander when I talk with a friend today, but with God's help, I'll remember that I need to hear what is said.

Perhaps we are just beginning to realize how fuzzy our values had become before we got into recovery. Being dependent on other people's approval was a way of life. We often vacillated on what we believed and how we behaved according to the person whose approval we sought.

We have new values to live by.

What a difference the Twelve Steps have made in our lives. With just a moment of daily reflection, we can act according to our new value system. It will require that we back away from our more habitual behaviors, but we can do it. And we have the support of friends who really want us to adopt this new set of principles wholeheartedly. It does make our lives simpler. When facing a situation that challenges us, we'll never again be at a loss about what's the right thing to do.

I am sure of how to think and act. I seek the approval of only God and myself today.

T^2

Why go to meetings?

The first time we hear that our <u>program</u> is not about getting people clean and sober, we question the point of going. But what we soon learn is that the program is for us, not for the addict or alcoholic. We learn that we deserve peace.

We'll think with greater clarity because Step One will help us give up our obsession with the alcoholic. From Steps Two and Three we'll develop a trust in a Higher Power and thus give up our fear. We'll finally give up a burden we've carried far too long when we come to believe it's not our job to get anyone sober. Our job is to find happiness and offer love to others. Nothing can better us more than this.

Time spent at meetings is never wasted. My happiness will be strengthened each time I use some part of the program.

Sometimes we want to hurt others. Maybe it's because we are feeling inadequate and jealous: We don't want them to get ahead of us, so we try to deflate their happiness. Maybe it's because they are not living up to our expectations. Or maybe it's because they continue using alcohol and other drugs, ignoring our pleas to stop. We may have dozens of reasons for wanting to inflict cruelty on others, but none is justified.

We can never take back our cruel words.

Learning the value of pausing, even for that brief moment before speaking, will bring us immediate rewards. Amends-making will be a simpler, less time-consuming task when we pause before responding to others. But more important, we will feel better about ourselves when we treat others with the respect they deserve. Every cruel word we inflict on another person will come back to us. So will every kindness. Furthermore, every time we show respect for others, we will be showered with greater respect too.

I can pause before I respond to people and remember respect is a two-way street.

*Compassion
doesn't mean
taking care of
people.*

Feeling compassion for a friend in pain is a loving way to respond. It softens the harsh edges of reality for the sufferer as well as for ourselves. Trying to take away the pain, however, is not appropriate. Each of us is on a journey of experiences and opportunities that will help us grow and fulfill God's plan for our lives. What we learn from the difficult steps we have to take is part of the plan.

It's not always easy to draw the line between showing compassion and trying to solve a friend's problem. Some of us have made it a practice to intrude on other people's lives. Neither they nor we have been helped by it. Learning how to maintain healthy boundaries between ourselves and others is part of our journey today. Practicing this kind of compassion will give us growth.

I will show compassion today by maintaining healthy boundaries and not intruding on other people's lives.

Why doesn't he just stop drinking? Can't she see the mess she is making of her life with drugs? How many times have we asked those questions? Only very gradually do we come to believe that our friends or loved ones are powerless over their <u>addiction.</u> They didn't snort cocaine the first time with the intention of becoming addicted, but over time it has happened.

Nobody wants to be addicted to drugs or alcohol.

Accepting their addiction is one of our assignments. Step One tells us we are *powerless,* and even if we understand the words, the concept is subtle and elusive. Why can't we influence them to change? It makes good sense, and it would improve their lives. Regular attendance at Twelve Step meetings like Al-Anon and many talks with a sponsor will help us realize how limited our power is over other people's actions. But we'll also learn how vast our power is over our own actions.

We are learning, perhaps reluctantly, to let others travel their own paths. Accepting <u>our powerlessness</u> and developing a belief that everyone has a Higher Power allow us to let go. This isn't easy, but we can do it. We are surrounded by others who have.

I may be as addicted to controlling others as they are to drugs. I will let the Steps help me today.

Letting go over and over: That's progress.

The first time we heard someone at a meeting say "Let go," we were confused. We had no idea what it meant or how to do it; even now, we forget on occasion. The people in our lives are special to us. And certainly for most of them, we want the very best. We've spent years trying to coach them. We've worried over their plights and relished their successes. We wonder how that can be wrong.

What we learn here is that prayers for loved ones are never wrong; however, trying to control, through any means, the thinking or the actions of anyone but ourselves is wrong. Letting go means letting others, those we love and those we barely know, do what they must.

Every day we'll have hundreds of opportunities to practice letting go. We'll get calls we don't want to handle, we'll meet people we don't want to know, we'll face situations we fear to address. Letting go of the people and the outcomes will become easier in time. The greater our progress, the deeper our happiness.

Most things that happen today will be out of my control. If I let go of them right away, I'll experience many peaceful hours.

Some days it may seem that all we do is give to other people. We may be giving our money and our time cleaning up the addict's messes, yet we receive no show of appreciation. Maybe we are always giving to friends too, trying to solve their problems, listening to their tales of woe, yet they're seldom there for us. If we're being used by others, let's assess how and why we have gotten involved in their lives. What are we giving, really? And what return are we expecting?

What comes to us is balanced by what we give.

HONEST INTENTIONS

An ancient spiritual maxim asserts that we will receive in direct measure to what we give. If we give hate, we'll receive meanness in return. Anger inspires anger.

And our attempts to control or manipulate will be seen for what they are. We are an open book. What's really in our hearts is what we're giving to others.

Deciding to feel love for people will make us more apt to love them. Our lesson is in realizing that giving love may mean letting those we have "taken care of" succeed or fail on their own.

I won't be doing other people a loving favor if I do for them what they need to do for themselves. God, help me be clearheaded before I give to others today.

Trusting our Higher Power makes it possible to receive help.

Being willing to ask for help is the first step in finding a solution to a problem. Next is to trust that our Higher Power is available and willing to help. Then we need to be open to the guidance that comes to us, sometimes through the quiet of our minds, sometimes through the words of a loving friend, sometimes through a passage in a treasured book.

We have come to this program because we are seeking help. And through the friends we meet here, we will find the solace and the solutions we need. The despair and hopelessness we may have felt in the past are lifted when we begin relying on a Higher Power for help. Following the example of the friends we meet will offer us changed lives and the peace that has eluded us for so long.

I will seek help even for tiny problems today. Getting used to looking to my Higher Power for guidance will make it easier for me to find.

No two people react alike to any one experience. Some of us are overly sensitive and get our feelings hurt, while a friend may not be bothered by the same experience. It's a revelation, perhaps, that we don't have to take most situations too seriously. We can choose to let most situations go with no residual effects, believing that they are one of our necessary lessons.

Suffering is usually optional.

OBJECTIVITY

Certain experiences will cause us pain, but feeling pain and suffering excessively are two very separate responses. We can begin to be more conscious of our responses to all experiences. We can come to appreciate how each experience contributes to the journey our Higher Power has planned for us. Being more conscious of our responses, we can step back and observe everything that happens to us. This gives us a healthier perspective.

I will take my journey in stride today and trust my Higher Power's plan for me.

Old habits are hard to break.

Our behavior and beliefs were ingrained by the time we entered the Twelve Step program. Our family of origin had taught us how to interpret our experiences. Our friends had complimented us for our values, or for the absence of them. So we had developed stock responses to many situations. We didn't think very hard or long about what to do. Unfortunately, we made many mistakes.

We are learning from those mistakes now, and we are slowly developing new responses. We are learning how to listen rather than how to shame or try to control. We are learning how to let other people make their own decisions. Seeking help from people who share this program is a big step for us. From the Steps we are absorbing a new set of values and a new understanding of who we really are. And we are trying to give our lives and will to God daily.

Our process for change will be a long one, but perfection is not expected. Making a tiny bit of progress, every day, is all that's necessary.

I can't change the things that need changing overnight. Just knowing that some habits need to go is a beginning. Today I'll work on one of them.

Having specific principles to guide us has given our lives new meaning. Measuring our actions and our goals against these principles has empowered us. No longer must we try to be like others because we aren't sure who we are. Every day we know ourselves a bit better.

For instance, we know now that it's far more comfortable to be honest with other people than it is to lie or even just to stretch the truth. Lying always kept us looking over our shoulders. Now, on our better days, we live our honesty by giving up some control, letting others make their own decisions (even when we're sure they are wrong), and letting God be in charge of *all* outcomes.

Our lives are simpler now. And we can be peaceful in every experience, since we've discovered we can rely on Twelve Step principles to serve us.

We are learning to "practice these principles in all our affairs."

STEP 12

So much of my guesswork about what to do here or there is gone, thankfully. Following the Twelve Step principles gives me my answer, always.

Our experiences depend on our outlook.

Doesn't everybody get mad at unruly children? Surely a downpour in the midst of an outing is depressing. And a job loss can't be anything but discouraging. Or can it? It's quite a revelation to note how differently each of us responds to our experiences. Seeing a glass as half-full rather than half-empty is clearly our decision.

Many of us have suffered from negative attitudes. Until we discovered a Twelve Step program, we didn't understand that it was within our power to relish all our experiences, to see them as points on our learning curve, to recognize that every experience is meant to bless our journey.

Life passes so quickly, and we have so much to learn along the way. Accepting every moment as sacred and just what we need relieves us of the tendency to judge experiences negatively.

Whatever comes to me today can be relished. I am "in process."

Forcing other people to accept our opinions, to live according to our rules, certainly doesn't bring us sustained happiness. Knowing that others resent our use of power taints any victory. But we exhibit our willfulness anyway and our relationships suffer.

Willfulness may win a battle but not the war.

We are in Al-Anon or other Twelve Step programs because our relationships are strained. We all want productive and peaceful relationships—that is, we want fun, relaxed times with others. But to have those times more than just occasionally, we must be willing to compromise when we aren't in agreement. And that takes maturity.

The Twelve Steps can help us mature. It's hard to give up fighting these unnecessary battles. The first three Steps will give us the guidance we need as we learn to let God resolve the struggles.

I will not struggle with anyone today. My peace of mind comes first.

We do not have to handle our problems alone.

Thinking that we needed no one's help made us feel strong and proud. We were capable, we were good managers, we had the answers. It's not easy to accept that our perceived ability to manage may well have been a facade for gross unmanageability and excessive control! Our attempts to handle the lives of too many people may have been our way of denying that other people had problems that were theirs to fix.

Help for solving problems comes wrapped in many dressings. Seeking help doesn't mean we have to let someone else force us to do something against our will. It does prove we're growing. We're learning that two heads are generally better than one, and we're coming to believe that wherever "two or more are gathered" God's presence will guide us.

We no longer will have to handle our problems alone if we seek the steady, loving guidance of sponsors, friends, and God. The real gift is that we'll feel strong once again, and we'll know why.

I will feel strong and capable today if I am willing to listen to others and to God when I have a problem to solve.

MAY

Even our closest friends seldom knew the details of the strife in our families. We frequently lied to bosses to cover up for absences, and we kept members of our family in the dark too. We were very good at making excuses, at covering up for the addict.

Genuine friendships develop within the rooms of this fellowship.

The men and women in these rooms can hear our honest voices and accept our pain without judgment. They understand our journey and can share their wisdom. Never before have we been so blessed with friendships as we are now. Never again do we need to feel alone with our troubles.

I now have friends who truly know me, all of me.
I will offer my friendship today to someone new.

*We can think
our way to
feelings
of love.*

NEGATIVE
REACTIONS

When we are agitated about or scared by the behavior of someone we love, we are letting unhealthy thoughts have control over our lives. Many of us do this quite regularly. We perhaps excuse it by saying "I can't help it." This is far from true, however.

The Twelve Steps are helping us understand what we are powerless over. Steps Four and Five make it clear what we are not powerless over. And at the top of that list are *thinking* and *feeling*. We can cultivate whatever thoughts we want. Our emotions are of our own making. When we get accustomed to this, we'll know an empowerment that will change our lives. Choosing to feel love, even in the midst of pain and chaos, is possible. After experiencing this awhile, we'll never want to return to our old ways of thinking.

The love I feel today is up to me. With each breath I will exhale love.

So many books have been written on "how to love" that many of us assume we don't know how and maybe will never learn. We can simplify the process, however, by focusing on the Golden Rule. For starters, we can treat others as respectfully as we'd like to be treated. People respond well to respect, and they often pay us respect in return.

Loving others begins with respect.

Next, let's put the needs of at least one other person ahead of our own today. It's imperative that we do it willingly, not resentfully. We can ask God to help us. We'll discover an unexpected benefit: Not being self-absorbed for a change is really quite refreshing.

Finally, we can ask God for freedom from the thinking that keeps us from loving others. Each person who enters our circle of experience today can be loved by us if we are willing to turn to God for help.

Loving others is easier if I keep it simple. I will focus on courtesy today.

The road to peace and sanity is available to us.

The first time we walked through the doors of a Twelve Step meeting we wondered how a gathering of ordinary people could possibly resolve the chaos in our lives. We'd tried every measure we could think of—to no avail. Spouses were still drunk, kids were out of control, and we felt hopeless, maybe even suicidal at times. How could these people help? we asked ourselves. Fortunately, we stayed, and a tiny miracle began to unfold.

It's hard to define how the program helps. But we agree it does. Certainly, it's helpful that we no longer feel isolated from others. It helps to know that others have faced similar trauma and survived. It also helps to be introduced to a loving Higher Power, since the God many of us grew up with was judgmental. Even more important, perhaps, is learning through the Fourth and Fifth Steps who we really are and what our part has been in the chaos of our lives.

Most importantly, we have learned that each day is another chance to live according to the values of this wonderful program. If yesterday we slipped into old behavior, we can try again today to be the person we really want to be.

I won't feel fearful, angry, or out of control today if I live according to the principles of this program.

Twelve Step recovery initially appealed to us because we wanted someone close to get sober. We thought that if we could do our part right, the other person would get sober. And we are learning our part: We have made concrete changes in how we think and what we do. However, the drinker may still be drinking. Recovery can change only us, not them.

Our purpose is not to get people sober.

RESPONSIBILITY

Living according to Twelve Step principles gives us a fresh perspective on life. Very few situations baffle us now. We have learned how to get quiet so we can hear our inner guide. We have learned to trust sponsors whose programs we admire. We have learned that it's not up to us to take charge of anyone else's life. Best of all, we have learned that all is well. No longer do we feel overwhelming hopelessness. Having hope for our lives makes each day full of promise.

I can be certain that every moment of this day will bless me in some way. Twelve Step principles will help me gain a fresh perspective.

Conflicts can be avoided.

ARGUING

We get into conflicts with other people because of us, not them. We can walk away from circumstances that are beginning to boil. We can decide that feeling peaceful is more important than forcing an opinion on someone else. And we can choose to seek God's guidance in every tense situation. Making these choices gets easier with practice, but at first we can't imagine not having the last word.

Many of us have too much invested in being right. Perhaps we think our worth relies on others' agreeing with our opinions. If we use the *right* words, a really good argument, we can sway their opinion, we hope. Sometimes we're successful. Unfortunately, that fuels our fire to push our opinion the next time too.

Deciding to accept that all people have a right to their opinion is a big change for us. Coming to believe that each of us is on a unique journey helps us make that decision.

The program is helping me understand other people. Today I'll walk away from every opportunity to argue with someone. The other person's perspective is as valid as my own.

Every Twelve Step group has a personality as unique as its members. Some groups are composed predominantly of women; others are a good mix of both sexes. And a few are exclusive to men or women. Because there are so many meetings available, at least in the larger communities, we can nearly always find one that's a good match for our needs. However, it's important to give a group a trial run of a few weeks before deciding whether it's the right group for us.

"Our leaders are but trusted servants."

GROUP PERSONALITY

The person leading the group may give an unfavorable impression initially. Again, it's important to stick around long enough to assess the group as a whole. The leader is a volunteer who has taken on a responsibility that benefits all of us. That person's particular bias, however, doesn't represent the group as a whole.

The reality is that we won't like every member of every group we attend. These meetings are no different from other gatherings we attend. However, we can learn to accept the contribution all members are making to our own growth simply by their presence at meetings that are changing our lives.

Leaving a group because I don't like one of its members is shortsighted. Sometimes we learn our most valuable lessons from people and situations we are uncomfortable with.

Accepting our power-lessness over other people relieves us of a heavy burden.

When we first hear the term *powerlessness,* we're baffled. What does it mean that we are powerless to control another person's behavior? With little or no success, we argued, manipulated, and cajoled. Our hours were filled with attempts to control.

Giving up this behavior is frightening at first. We might ask ourselves, what do we do now? At length, we learn through the example of others to live for ourselves. Though it may have seemed selfish at first, we are realizing a new freedom that energizes us. We are beginning to glimpse the richness of our own lives now that we have time to focus on *us.*

I will relish my freedom from the lives of loved ones today. I'll focus on my behavior only.

Understanding what we want from a relationship and articulating it is appropriate and healthy. Sharing our expectations about a job or a friendship tells us who we are and allows others to know us too. For many of us, however, clearly defining who we are and what we want are new behaviors. Passively letting others define us, as had been our custom, took us off the hook. It gave us permission to blame *them* when *our* lives didn't work. Now we can see how that kept us down and made us feel powerless, perhaps even hopeless.

When we stand up for ourselves we take responsibility for our needs.

ASSERTIVENESS

Standing up for ourselves is empowering. And exhilarating! Doing it respectfully enhances our well-being. Because it is new behavior, we may need lots of dry runs before we figure out how to avoid aggressiveness while taking responsibility for ourselves. Our repeated attempts will pay off.

I will decide what I want and need from other people today. By sharing that information, I will respect all of us.

*Easy
Does It.*

Our impatience makes us anxious and agitated. It often causes conflicts with other people too. We want what we want, when we want it! Perhaps we fail to believe that the experiences we need will come to us when the time is right.

All we have is right now. The people we're sharing our lives with deserve our full attention and love. It's from them, all of them, that we get our lessons and messages from God. Our interactions are part of our specific journey, and the more serenely we handle them, the more we'll get from each experience.

Taking Easy Does It as our motto for how we live will change how we perceive every experience. The anger over a spouse who still drinks or a child who's rebellious will be lessened if we get quiet momentarily and focus on the motto Easy Does It. We say we want freedom from pressure, that we are tired of the stress in our lives. We can change them, instantly; it's all a matter of choice. Remembering easy does it, does it.

I can be free of every pressure. Three simple words can change my experiences today. Easy does it *will be my prayer.*

Keeping silent while a friend is talking should not be confused with <u>listening</u>. Dialogue can fill our minds even when friends are sharing the most intimate details of their lives. Why is it so difficult to listen?

To listen is to hear with one's heart.

Our listening impairment probably began in childhood. We feared we didn't measure up, so we were constantly obsessed with what other people thought of us. Worry became a way of life, and we seldom distinguished between the trivial and the important. We learned to keep our minds trapped in thought.

Listening with our heart is a new skill. When we try it, we'll first be touched by the emotion contained in the message being shared. Then our own worry thoughts will recede. Letting another's pain or joy reach our hearts will enrich us. We will come to understand that paying loving attention to someone's story will offer us answers we didn't even know we needed.

It's not coincidental if a friend comes to me in need today. I'll receive the guidance I need through what is shared.

Detachment is always possible.

We can take our feelings and our minds on a "mini-trip" every time the people in our lives get abusive or the circumstances in our lives get too demanding. But we don't have to deny our emotions and let others control how we feel and what we do. For many of us, this is an astonishing revelation. We never understood how able we really were to decide what we would feel.

Detachment sounds more mysterious than it really is. At first we may think it means we can't care about our loved ones anymore. Actually, letting others alone to do what they will and practicing acceptance are far more caring. Detaching is acknowledging that each of us is responsible for our own journey.

My journey will be what I make it today. I will detach with love.

We can never know, absolutely, what <u>God's plan</u> for our lives is. Yet we can trust that there is one and that we are being watched over. Almost every day an experience troubles us. Maybe it's a phone call from a drunk friend or criticism from a boss. So quickly we judge its meaning for our lives. But from the experiences we were certain we couldn't live through we garnered important knowledge and growth. <u>Today's experiences too will be understood in time.</u>

We can find value in most experiences.

Because we don't know just where God is taking us, we can't possibly anticipate all that we'll need to know. That's where God's plan comes in. We will be given our lessons when the time is right. We won't be led into situations we're unprepared for. And we'll have to trust that each circumstance we do face is necessary and part of our unfolding.

When we wonder, why me? let's remember how lucky we are to still be fulfilling God's plan.

My recovery is as much a part of God's plan as was my obsessive codependency. I'm in a position to help other people now. Today's interactions will lend purpose to my life.

Staying in the present diminishes worries.

Worrying about tomorrow or next year distracts our focus from this moment, and this moment is all God has assured us. Practicing the Third Step every day relieves us of worry about the future. God will be present in whatever future we are given. That's a promise! Admittedly, it's hard to give up worrying. It's what we did for years. But we can give it up. And we can give up our problems too.

Nothing can really frighten us if we live our lives one breath at a time. Breathing in the presence of our Higher Power extinguishes the flame of fear that worry triggers. Hearing others share experiences "proving" this to be true, we will gain the hope to try it too.

The next time a loved one uses drugs or a boss blames us for a problem, we'll remember that God can be counted on to see us through the experience. We'll come to believe that we can let every future circumstance be handled in its own time too.

I will be free of worry today if I use the Third Step and believe that God will take care of me.

Reflecting on how we behaved during our most trying times with the alcoholic in our lives helps us see how much we have grown. We frequently acted vengefully and even more often resentfully. And we felt justified. After all, we had told the alcoholic to stop!

How much we have learned since then. We have come to accept alcoholism as a disease, and we realize that we are affected by the other person's illness too. Using these Twelve Steps has made it possible for us to behave more lovingly, certainly more sanely, than before. We can check out our thinking and our plans for action with others before doing anything, often saving ourselves from unnecessary conflict.

We can be fairly certain that the excessive turmoil of earlier periods is over. Working our own program, letting the others in our lives work theirs, assures us of that. What a wonderful gift clear thinking is.

Thinking clearly, sanely, is one of the rewards from working these Twelve Steps.

CLARITY

I will share my gratitude for my sanity with someone else today. Perhaps my sharing will inspire that person to seek a better life too.

*Our
principles
determine
our behavior.*

THINKING
FOR
OURSELVES

Giving other people power over our actions, and not respecting or remembering our own values, is part of *our* problem. If she uses drugs again, we get mad and hurt. If he fails to come home when promised, we get anxious and imagine the worst. For years, perhaps, we have let the behavior of others control how we feel and what we do. We simply reacted without thinking.

Our friends in the program remind us there is another way to live. We can decide how *we* want to act. Pausing for a moment before reacting to any affront or situation will give us a chance to take charge of ourselves and thus our actions. In the process, we'll begin redefining or recalling the values that are important to us. Learning to live by our values will simplify every action we'll take today.

Going to my own core for guidance on who I will be today will help me to know peace.

We caused many problems for ourselves because we tried to control other people. When we entered Twelve Step programs, we were fairly certain that our attempts were justified. We expected to get support for our efforts from the people in our groups. After all, they knew what it was like living with addiction.

Twelve Step programs are not havens for controllers.

What a surprise is in store for us. From the very first meeting we discover that controlling others, or at least trying to, is never acceptable. The only person we have the liberty to control is ourselves. How can we close our eyes to the irresponsible actions of others? we wonder. With patience, we come to understand that recovery is dependent on each of us assuming personal responsibility.

Giving up our need to control takes vigilant effort. Daily work on the first three Steps of the program builds the foundation for giving up control. God will take charge, guiding us as well as them, when we give up control. Only then can the changes we've hoped for happen.

I can give up my controlling ways if I'm willing to accept that a Higher Power might know what's best.

Perfection, like beauty, is in the eye of the beholder.

Is the desire to be perfect keeping us from being our best? Are mistakes okay? Trial and error is how *healthy* people learn. However, our expectation of perfection when we make a first attempt keeps us frustrated, or maybe we are too fearful of failure to even start. We waste so much *living* wanting to be perfect that we fear to try anything new.

Because we suffer from the need to be perfect, we judge other people harshly too. Perfection quickly becomes the bane of our existence. Fortunately, we can ask our Higher Power and the friends in our groups to help us accept ourselves as less than perfect human beings. We'll be able to do this with greater ease when we learn to accept others as they are.

I will be good enough at every activity today if I simply do the best I can.

It's only human to think we're always right and to assume others need enlightenment. Many unnecessary arguments follow. The more familiar we become with the principles of this program, the easier it will be to respect that others have <u>opinions</u> too. Sharing our view is one thing; trying to force it on someone else is quite another!

Our words, unless loving, need not be spoken.

Since joining this fellowship, we have been exposed to so many new tools, one of which is keeping our thoughts and opinions, unless loving, to ourselves. This tool wields significant impact. It changes how we are perceived. Even more importantly, it changes how we perceive others. To look through eyes that are loving, and to speak words that reflect *that* view, changes every moment of our lives every day.

I can be a person even I'd look up to today. It's all a matter of how I speak and what I say.

Helping other people sustains the miracle of recovery.

T STEP
TWELVE →

If others had not been present to help us when we attended our first meeting, we'd still be fighting all the old battles: doing for loved ones what they need to do for themselves; "guilting" them about their continued drug use; worrying incessantly about how to change them; worrying about their behavior and what other people think.

The understanding and comfort we found in the program made our burdens lighter instantly. Knowing that we were not alone, that others had lived through similar experiences, was the first moment of relief we'd felt in years. It's our turn now to offer the same hope and comfort to others.

And now we understand that we profit too each time we lend a supporting arm or ear to a newcomer. Sharing our message with others guarantees us of God's active role in our lives. That's the real miracle of the Twelve Step path.

I want to give back some of what I've been given. Today will present me with opportunities. God, help me see them.

Who doesn't have some guilt? Surely no one we know has been "good" all the time. It's human to make mistakes and hurt others in the process. On occasion, we have even intentionally harmed someone. We can't undo the past. What's done is done. However, we can get free of the inhibiting shadow it casts over our lives today if we use the tools of this program of recovery.

Guilt keeps us stuck.

AMENDS

The first step in shedding our guilt is to admit to ourselves that some of the things we have done are wrong. The next step is harder. We need to admit our wrongdoing to the one we have harmed and ask for his or her forgiveness. This can be made easier if we remember to bring along our Higher Power.

Why is all this necessary? As long as we have wounds in our relationships, we won't be able to see all the possibilities for growth and change that beckon us today. Our guilt keeps us stuck in the past, and it's the present that promises us the happiness we desire.

How are my relationships today? Do any feel tense because of my past behavior? If I really want to get the most from what today offers, I need to mend the past. With God's help I can.

We can untangle our lives from those of our loved ones.

Alcoholism or other drug addiction in our families caused us to take on other people's responsibilities. Our lives became a pattern of reactions. Whatever others did determined what we did. However they felt controlled what we felt. We transferred this response to many outside the family too.

Today we know that respecting the boundaries between us and others takes willingness and perseverance. It may have seemed nearly impossible at first: We simply didn't know how to think of ourselves as separate human beings. But now we can rely on the example of others and ask our sponsors for guidance. Others who have come to recovery programs have felt similar frustration, yet they have made progress. We too will make progress.

If I have any doubt today about what is my responsibility and what is clearly someone else's, I'll ask my sponsor.

Very few of us came into the program filled with joy and serenity. Most of us came as a last resort! We were anxious about the future, about the using behavior of someone close, about our own capabilities, about the decisions we needed to make. Mostly, our focus was negative, perhaps even hopeless.

Serenity is a gift available to us all if we want it.

What a wonderful choice we have made. The program can change our lives, just as it has changed the lives of all the people in the program. We have to put forth some effort, of course, and we have to willingly let a Higher Power take control of our lives and the outcomes of our experiences. The result will be a measure of serenity that is new to us, a serenity quickly treasured.

The Serenity Prayer will help us to maintain our new perspective when we are wavering on what to do in the old, all too familiar situations. Some things we can always change—that's where our effort comes in. Other things are not up to us—that's where God comes in. Listening for God's guidance teaches us the difference.

I will rely on the Serenity Prayer and will listen for guidance every time I'm confused today.

Just for today we can handle anything.

T²
LIVING IN THE PRESENT

Our lives are frightening at times. Conflict with significant people causes fear of abandonment. A new job triggers fear of inadequacy. Family counseling is just beginning and we want to back out. Perhaps we simply had a bad dream that seemed far too real. Any of these reasons might push our "fear" button, but we *can* handle anything if we ask God for help and take it one day at a time.

Most of us, however, live in the future, whether that means this evening or next week. Yet when we stick with this moment only, and then ask God to be with us, we learn that we can handle anything today.

We feel free and confident when we remember that this twenty-four hours is all we have, and nothing will happen that can't be taken care of by our Higher Power.

My life will not be frightening even once today if I keep my mind on God.

In Al-Anon and other Twelve Step programs we are exposed to ideas that seem foreign. It takes time to realize this is an entirely new value system, one that we can live by every day, not just the days we go to meetings. Absorbing these principles and then using them as guides for every decision and action remove the worry and guesswork from our lives. How can the program be this simple?

Living the Twelve Step way is a 24-hour-a-day opportunity.

COMMITTMENT TO TWELVE STEPS

Changing how we've thought and acted doesn't happen overnight. Changing one thing at a time is enough at first. Perhaps we'll give up our feeling of hopelessness. The Second Step tells us that God can free us from our insanity, *our hopelessness.* All we need do is ask for help, and hope will come. Maybe we decide the urge to take over someone else's life must end. Doing and redoing the First Step numerous times a day will help us remember that we are powerless over everyone else. If discomfort from an old relationship keeps haunting us, maybe it's time to make amends and get on with life.

Every part of our lives is influenced by the value system we adhere to. Adopting Twelve Step philosophy as our own simplifies our lives, particularly when the baggage of the past has been cleared away.

This isn't a part-time program for me. I want to live by these principles every minute. My life will reflect how successfully I do it.

We can allow other people their own journeys.

Accepting that each of us has a specific "mission," a unique journey on this earth, frees us to focus on our own lives. It's not always easy, however. We may be drawn to others' pain. We may worry about the unnecessary conflicts in their lives. We may feel the impact of their irresponsibility far too often. But we must remember, again and again, that whatever they do is not for us to judge. Our mission is not to change them or their journey. We can change only our focus.

Letting go of others gives us time that we may not know how to utilize initially. We have grown accustomed to worrying about others, and it has controlled our behavior and thoughts. And at first, being free of anxiety leaves us feeling empty. How lucky for us that we have the Second and Third Steps to guide us through this period of adjustment. It's quite a change to focus on our journey only. Our Higher Power is waiting to guide us.

I must let others walk their own path today. God will help me walk mine if I ask for guidance.

We learn early in this program that we are powerless over all the people we have been trying to control. If they want to do drugs, they will. We are powerless over all the circumstances of their lives too. If they get fired from a job or go to jail, we aren't at fault. But most importantly, we are coming to understand that we aren't powerless when it comes to our own lives.

Growing up in this program means no longer getting to blame others for how we behave. Taking full responsibility for our attitudes, our thinking, and our behaviors may overwhelm us at first. But in time taking responsibility heightens our self-esteem. And many of us need that. We'll look forward to every opportunity for responsible action, because we can subtly feel ourselves growing and changing each time we take charge of ourselves.

We feel a healthy sense of power when we accept responsibility for all of our actions.

SELF TO
RESPONSIBILITY

I will appreciate my opportunities for growing up today. I'll have many of them!

Reacting too quickly to any situation, grave or mundane, can lead us astray. Only by pausing first to hear God's suggestion can we be certain of doing the right thing or saying what's best. Somebody has to be willing to back away from an ugly conflict, or it can turn violent. Let's be the ones. The program has given us the tools, and we'll gain in the process. We'd never have won the war anyway.

Taking a time-out will benefit everyone.

RESTRAINT

T²
THINK BEFORE
TALKING/
ACTING

Arguments are normal—healthy, even. We all see circumstances from unique perspectives; thus disagreements ensue. How we represent these perspectives is a sign of how much we have grown, and the opportunities for more growth will present themselves daily.

Learning that we have the choice to back away is powerful information. It makes peace possible.

I'll be quiet rather than argumentative today. The change will feel wonderfully peaceful.

The idea of getting emotional support from people we hardly know astounds us. For most of our lives we didn't let others know what we were feeling or experiencing. We assumed they'd judge us and gossip about our shortcomings. Thus to share all of who we are with women and men whose last names we don't even know seems crazy at first.

It doesn't take many meetings, however, to recognize the genuine love and support that group members express to one another. Their tales of woe are often far graver than our own experiences, yet they smile. They seem at peace. They know their friends in these rooms will help them shoulder their burden. Nothing has to be handled alone, in isolation, without the love, acceptance, and guidance that are the hallmarks of a Twelve Step program. And now this is our privilege too. All our todays will be easier with the support of our Twelve Step friends.

Emotional support makes all experiences survivable.

I am guaranteed the help and support I want. All I have to do is ask for it. I'll make a call today.

Chemical dependency is a misunderstood disease.

OTHER
PEOPLES
PERCEPTIONS

Not everybody understands that alcoholism or other drug addiction is a disease. Before coming to the program many of us didn't understand that either. We reacted to the lies, the drunkenness, and the fights with hurt feelings and, occasionally, with rage. "Why didn't you stop drinking before you got drunk?" we asked hundreds of times, but nothing changed.

We know why now, because we understand the nature of chemical dependency. Once we have this education, we may want other people to quickly accept chemical dependency as a disease, rather than a moral issue.

Because of our love for the alcoholic or addict, we may want to change how others perceive that person. Fortunately, we have the First Step to remind us that we are powerless. We can work on changing only ourselves, not the alcoholic or addict, not friends, not strangers who might think chemical dependency is a moral issue. Sharing what we have learned about alcoholism through the program is all we can do to educate others.

Although I can't change how others choose to see the alcoholic or addict in my life, I can use my understanding of chemical dependency as a disease to educate others today.

Being overly concerned with or involved in others' lives is a symptom of codependency. Our feelings about ourselves have too often been dependent on our relations with others. Now we're working to change that.

We can be free of turmoil and frustration.

A key element of recovery is learning to detach from the affairs of others. Making sure a partner goes to work is not our responsibility. Smoothing relations between a parent and a sibling is not our job. Making excuses for a loved one's drunken behavior doesn't help that person get help. Our *best* response is no response in every situation where another's behavior is causing problems.

It's very hard to quit helping when a friend is in trouble. Fortunately, we have the example of other people in the program to follow.

Today I can recognize the boundaries between me and others. How they behave is not my concern, and it's not my job to fix it.

JUNE

Efficiency is great! Accomplishments are too. Being responsible and accountable are notable qualities. But demanding too much responsibility, accountability, and efficiency of ourselves puts us on an activity treadmill that steals our peace of mind. When we try to manage *everything*, we soon feel overwhelmed, and our self-esteem plummets.

Trying to manage too much makes our lives unmanageable.

MANAGEABILITY

Getting well in this program means discovering that we don't have to *do* anything to be okay. We don't have to *be* good managers to be worthy. Taking responsibility for our actions is still necessary, but our Higher Power loves us regardless of how much we get done today. Our only real "assignment" is to love and be thoughtful of other people all day long.

If I can manage my actions toward others today, I will have done enough. That assignment I can handle.

JUNE 2

Tomorrow will take care of itself.

A gift of this program is learning that we only have to handle *today*. Another gift is knowing that God will never give us more than we can handle. Acceptance of these two gifts will change our lives. How grateful we are becoming that we have the example of so many friends in the program to help us understand how to use these gifts.

Worrying about what may never happen next week or even next year was commonplace for many of us. It never occurred to us to think only of this day.

By contrast, being focused on here, now, means not being habitually obsessed about the what-ifs. It may seem irresponsible at first to give up our focus on the tomorrows. How can they unfold if we aren't paying attention to them? Only when we get accustomed to living this day, however, do we find relief. It's a whole new way of seeing life, and it makes our journey easier.

These twenty-four hours are all we have—for now. Whatever my Higher Power gives me to-day will be right for my journey.

Having a balanced view of ourselves is one of our goals in recovery. Typically, though, our shortcomings are more obvious than our assets, particularly to others: We're bossy. We're pouty and manipulative. We're shaming. But we have many positive traits too. Fortunately, the Fourth Step asks us to give attention to our whole self, to our assets along with our defects.

We are much more than our defects.

INVENTORIES

Discerning our assets may seem difficult, perhaps because our faults are more glaring. However, acknowledging our strengths is a key to growth. Let's remember yesterday. What did we do that we were proud of? What behavior felt right and pleased others? Taking pen to paper and detailing our positive actions help us recognize who we are in a broader sense. This is all the Fourth Step means. There is no mystery to it. It's far less difficult than most of us make it. And it's far more rewarding.

Before going to bed I will do a brief inventory of my behavior. Knowing who I really am is important to me.

Our bruised egos often push us to respond to other people in hurtful, thoughtless ways. Yet taking a moment to remember that everyone touched by an event has a different perspective helps us remain silent when our egos want to scream.

We can learn to control our reactions.

ARGUING

Deciding who is right and who is wrong wastes many precious moments every twenty-four hours. What we can learn in the program is that no one has to be right or wrong. We can decide, instead, that we'd rather be peaceful and let others have their own opinions.

We experience a rush of exhilarating freedom each time we back away from an unnecessary confrontation. The first few times we back away we may be uncomfortable, because arguing had become our habit. But we can make a habit too of not arguing. Serenity and empowerment will be the rewards.

No one makes me argue. I have chosen to. Today I will be quiet and peaceful and let others have their own opinions.

False pride keeps us stuck in old behavior and unnecessary pain. Why is it so hard to acknowledge who we really are? Do we think it's a secret? We can be assured that admitting our failings to another person and to God, as suggested by the Fifth Step, won't be startlingly new information to either.

Secrets keep us walled in.

Until we have done this Step we cannot fathom the relief we will feel. Our secrets have constricted us. Our obsession with them has stolen our peace of mind and our creativity. We are much more than our defects, but we can't see that until we have unburdened ourselves of them.

After revealing it all, we see that we're not so different from everyone else. The person we've chosen to hear our Fifth Step doesn't bat an eye at even the worst of our transgressions. Any expectation we might have had that God would punish us vanishes. We know now that God has always known who we are. And we are coming to believe that we have been loved unconditionally all along.

Why am I so afraid of telling who I really am? I'll take a chance by telling someone at least one small secret today and see what happens.

Accepting help is easier if we are humble.

Having humility is not the same as being humiliated. Some of us confused the two when we first came into the Twelve Step program. Living with addiction in the home or workplace meant regularly being humiliated. We experienced defeat, unwarranted criticism, unending emotional abuse. And our egos suffered. But that's not humility.

Humility means surrendering our ego, our certainty that we have the answer, and seeking, instead, the counsel of our Higher Power or friends we trust. Only when we let our ego rest can we hear the words of wisdom other people offer. We needed their wisdom or we wouldn't have ended up here.

We've had lots of pain in our lives. We'll no doubt experience more pain, but accepting help will make the experiences tolerable, and we won't be defeated. Humbly asking our Higher Power for help guarantees we'll get it.

My friends get on their knees when they really want God to hear them. If I feel scared or alone at any time today, I'll follow their example.

We have made habits of the more mundane activities: brushing our teeth, combing our hair, setting our alarm clocks. We forget, however, that even the simplest of our daily rituals were once unknown to us. Today we can begin making habits of more important actions. Being willing to love, ourselves and others, is one example. This can become another of our daily rituals, one that will heap wonderful rewards upon us.

Making the decision to love gets easier with practice.

Why is it so hard to love? Maybe it's that we feel vulnerable, at risk—we think if love isn't returned, we'll feel diminished. But by thinking this way we have complicated the *idea* of love. Instead, we can believe we have always been loved, unconditionally, by our Higher Power. This belief can take away some of our fear of loving others. In the program we are learning that love is another word for acceptance. If we simplify love for ourselves, we can remove some of its mystery. Soon we'll discover that we can show love as easily as we can say hello.

I will be "accepting" and thus cultivate feelings of love at every opportunity today.

To detach is to trust our journey.

Each of us has a Higher Power for guidance as we travel our unique journey through life. If we get too involved with another person's problems, we hinder the journey that person needs to make. We aren't the other person's Higher Power. To back away, to detach, is really the most loving thing we can do. It's letting the other person find a unique path; it's letting that person grow and change in the ways that fulfill his or her purpose.

We may resist detachment now, because we used to get self-worth from caretaking others. We mistakenly thought that caretaking others was essential to our journey. It never was. But showing support and offering love and prayers are. We are learning to see what is in the best interests of all recovering people, those who are chemically dependent and those of us who love them.

I will be loving, but I won't do for other people what they need to do for themselves today.

Conflict can result from trying to change a person or situation that we don't like. And conflict causes stress and agitation, both of which limit our lives. They steal our ability to be open to opportunities for growth and change.

Acceptance frees us.

Why is it so hard to accept situations we don't like? Twelve Step programs tell us it's because of our ego. We feel diminished when others don't agree with our plan or our opinion. Our self-worth is tied to other people's reactions.

But we can change. We can let the success stories we hear in this program inspire us to let others be. We will discover how much better we feel when we're not on the battlefield with our friends and loved ones.

I don't have to have conflict with other people today. I can let others be themselves and do what feels right to them. I'll feel more at ease too.

Surrendering to God's caring plan eases our walk today.

When first introduced to the idea that a Higher Power is in charge of our lives, the lives of our loved ones, and all the situations we've struggled so hard to control, we balk. We don't want to turn over the reins to anyone. After all, how can we be certain our loved ones will stop drinking if we quit pleading? Or who is going to make sure the children don't get into drugs if we aren't nagging them about their friends and their whereabouts all the time?

How lucky we are to have discovered, at last, the peace that comes with surrendering. There is a plan for our lives. There is a plan for our companion's life too. And for our friends' and associates' lives. No one of us has been left out of the divine plan. But we couldn't see this before. We were too intent on trying to run lives as though we were all-powerful. Now we can breathe easier, knowing God will take care of all those people we tried to manage but couldn't.

As Step Three suggests, I will turn my will and my life over to God today and enjoy these twenty-four hours.

Many of us believe in God. Most cultures in this world, in fact, believe in a supreme being. But simply believing in a Higher Power is not the same as being spiritually awake.

Formally, *spiritually awake* means having a two-way relationship with God. Informally it means having a friendship that keeps our hope for a better life alive.

Now we no longer pray to a distant, unseen God. We talk, each day, with the God of our understanding.

Being active in the most important relationship we have is what keeps us awake spiritually. That, in turn, is what fosters every positive change, every aspect of growth we experience.

What does it mean to be "awakened T2 *spiritually"?*

PRAYER

My chat with God today will keep me on track and firm in my understanding of the power of God's presence.

Every experience can benefit us if we believe in its value.

LESSONS

Growing up in an abusive family or suffering through a painful marriage seems far too traumatic to be considered beneficial. Even when a trusted friend in the program tells us that no experience is without a silver lining, we resist believing at first. Eventually, though, as we learn to rely on the principles of this program, the clarity that comes offers us a new perspective. We can finally see that even the most difficult of our experiences taught us valuable lessons we might never have otherwise learned.

This awareness is worth a lot. It allows us to let go of the past. And it allows us to forgive our abusive "teachers" and recognize that their personal torment controlled their behavior.

The negative experiences in my past served a purpose. I will come to believe in their value, and I will trust that all my experiences today are right for me now. My Higher Power will help me through them.

When someone close to us such as a spouse, partner, or friend drinks excessively, we can distance ourselves physically and emotionally. The physical separation is easier, of course. But the emotional separation is what gives our spirit relief.

The behavior of others does not have to control us.

It's normal to try to control the behavior of someone we care about. We may even want to control the behavior of people we don't know! Likewise, we let others' behavior control us. Instead, we can choose to seek a healthy emotional and physical distance and thus maintain our well-being. Remembering this and asking God for the help to do it will bring us peace.

I will seek distance whenever I need it today in order to honor my spirit.

We hear what works at good meetings.

Newcomers at meetings often need the guidance of old-timers regarding what's appropriate for discussion. Because of the severe pain some of us are in, we may feel compelled to talk about the drinker. A sponsor can help us by explaining "how it works" at meetings and the role sponsors play in our lives to get us on the right track.

We come to meetings because we all need continuing guidance and frequent reminders of how the Steps work in our lives. It is extremely easy to fall back into old behavior. Listening to how other people use a Step or a slogan is often the very help we need to prevent a slide backwards.

I'll keep growing and changing as long as I am in the program. Helping others gives me practice in using what I have learned.

Our judgments of other people may be blatant or subtle. When our judgments are blatant, we can recognize them, know that we aren't loving unconditionally, and consciously focus on letting the judgments go. More often, however, our thoughts are subtle and so much harder to let go of. But letting go is a goal we can strive for. Every experience with another person allows us an opportunity to love unconditionally, free of judgment.

Unconditional love means total acceptance, free of all judgment.

T2

JUDGING OTHERS

Our judgments of others generally reflect how we feel about ourselves at the time. When we are in tune with our spiritual center and feeling confident, we are comfortable with others too. Going within ourselves is a tool we can use for getting free of our judgments. When they begin to shadow our thoughts, we can go within and find God and freedom.

My judgment of others is a barometer of how close I am to my Higher Power today. Prayer will help me love others and myself.

Changing what we can is essential.

We come into this program exasperated because our attempts to change others have failed. We'd been certain that if the drinker stopped drinking and the boss quit nagging and the kids settled down, we'd be happy and secure. However, none of the above happened. Our subsequent desperation brought us to the program, and now good fortune is beginning to strike.

The first valuable lesson we learn is that we can't change anyone else, no matter how lofty our motives or how domineering our personality. Screaming, pouting, pleading, bartering, crying, or leaving won't make other people change. If they change, it's because they have decided to change, not because we won.

Our second valuable lesson is that *we* can change. We can change what we expect of others. We can decide to let a Higher Power guide our actions. We can "lighten up." We can focus our attention on this day only. We can trust that there is a plan for our lives and that all is well.

There is a lot I can do today. I'll begin by keeping my attention on my behavior and working on my relationship with God.

Taking a careful look at our own behavior is not as easy as keeping track of someone else's behavior. Most of us had lots of practice keeping track of someone else's behavior for many years. Now we can carefully document our own behavior. An unexpected reward is discovering that we have many positive qualities to go with our shortcomings. Many of us would fail to appreciate our assets if it weren't for doing an inventory.

Doing an inventory does not need to overwhelm us. Keeping it simple will keep it manageable. Perhaps we should look at yesterday or last week, rather than our whole lives. We'll know who *we* are if we honestly admit to how we treated other people. And be assured that many times we will like who we are!

"Made a searching and fearless inventory . . ."

SELF
AWARENESS

T2
STEP FOUR

Paying attention to who I am today will give me opportunities to see how I may want to change. I may also see reasons to feel proud.

Controlling other people never works.

How many precious hours have we wasted trying to <u>control</u> the behavior of a loved one? Were we successful? It's doubtful. At least not for the long term. We simply have no power to make other people act against their will.

Why are we driven to try? Generally, because we are certain that *our* way of living and doing is the right way. But the fact of the matter is, every one of us has a unique journey to make. The best we can offer one another are prayers for safety and the willingness to follow God's will. Through the principles of this program we are learning, at long last, that letting God control the "uncontrollables" is a good decision.

I may be right about how a friend should live life, but it's not in my power to control outcomes. I'll back off every time I get too pushy today.

Many of us came into the program very practiced in prayer. We prayed for God to change our lives, or at least the alcoholic's life. We prayed that our future would be different from our present or our past. In our hopelessness, however, we felt abandoned by God. We seldom felt a relationship with God. That's what we are discovering now.

Being good at talking to God isn't enough. The rest of the equation is <u>listening</u> for the response, for the subtle nudge, or simply for the silence because the time for action is not at hand. Talking and listening, praying and waiting—these are the components of this relationship we hope to cultivate. And even if we can't *see* God, we still can *hear* what our next step should be. But until we learn to get quiet and listen, we'll never enjoy the relationship we crave, the relationship that promises to change our lives in every wonderful way.

A relationship with God, as with everyone else, is both give and take.

GUIDANCE

My <u>relationships</u> with friends work because we talk and listen to each other. Today I will remember that God can become the best friend I'll ever have if I treat this relationship likewise.

Life is like a boomerang. What we send out comes flying back to us.

RECIPROCATING
EMOTIONS

Every one of us wants expressions of love and acceptance from our friends, family, even our co-workers, and we are learning that we can influence how other people treat us. While it's true we can't control them, we can, in most cases, expect treatment that's equal to what we offer.

That's powerful information to have at our disposal. Being acutely aware of the signals we send to other people, and making sure those signals are kind and well-meaning, mean that we'll seldom be confronted with the harsh, critical responses we perhaps are used to receiving.

We are learning so much about healthy relationships since joining this fellowship. Having hope for change, for our very lives, in fact, is more common to us now than ever before. Hallelujah!

I am fairly certain of the kind of treatment I'll get from others today. It will match what I dish out.

We can anticipate the day we have awakened to with a feeling of promise or dread. There will be situations, no doubt, that we'd rather not face. Petty irritations may shadow us part of the day, but most likely we'll find a few circumstances to laugh over. We will find more of these circumstances if we so choose. The attitude we have today will determine the quality of our day.

If only we knew how many days we were guaranteed, it might not matter so much what we did with just one of them. But we don't know. These twenty-four hours we awakened to today are ours to make the most of. And we can make each one of them pleasant and memorable, or very miserable. Letting someone else's behavior determine how we experience our own day can be disastrous. We know this from the pain we had in our lives prior to finding this program.

Each moment of these twenty-four hours is unique and will never come again.

LIVING IN THE PRESENT

I will find as much joy in today as I want to find. I will try to remember that each moment is sacred and full of promise.

What goes around comes around.

EXPECTATIONS

We think we have so little <u>control</u> over the people and events surrounding us. But we do have some control. The fact is, *whatever we give to others often comes back to us.* If we give them love and respect, we'll often receive that. If we are shaming and mean-spirited, that will come to us too. Our actions influence how others treat us.

Not everyone, however, can or is willing to return our caring and respect. When our best intentions backfire with people who are still drinking or using other drugs, we need to remember that we can't control their reactions and behaviors. What we can control are our own reactions.

I can give love today, and that act will show respect for myself as well as others.

Letting someone else's behavior determine how we feel at every turn is irresponsible. Our emotions should be determined by *us*, not by someone else. But no doubt we have spent years confusing the boundaries that separate us from other people. Whether at work or at home, we have too often let someone else's "insanity" affect how we behave and how we feel.

Detachment *means "freedom from emotion."*

At first, it may seem insensitive not to react to others' problems or negative behavior. We may fear they'll think we simply don't care about them. Learning that it is far more caring to let other people handle their own lives takes time and patience. But with practice, it will begin to feel comfortable. In fact, in time it will feel freeing and wonderful.

I will work on detachment today, knowing that in time the rewards will come.

Program friendships are special.

Until we came into the program we may have thought that friendships were all alike. We counted on friends to socialize and gossip with, maybe to share a secret with. But when we were really scared about our lives and the future, we felt too vulnerable to let anyone else know our innermost thoughts.

What relief the program has brought us, and what good friends! No problem seems as terrifying now that we are no longer shouldering it alone. Having to make a decision no longer overwhelms us when we have other people to discuss it with. Letting ourselves be deeply cared for, with all our faults, is a new experience too. All these gifts come automatically to us within the fellowship. All that is asked of us is that we be a friend too.

I will extend my heart in friendship today, and my concerns will be lightened.

Some of us exaggerate small setbacks, making our lives far more complicated than necessary. Instead, we need to nurture a positive outlook. The wise among us say, "It's all in how you look at it."

A negative attitude creates problems, not opportunities.

Acknowledging our negative attitude is the first step to discovering happiness. As Humboldt said, "I am more and more convinced that our happiness or unhappiness depends far more on the way we meet the events of life, than on the nature of those events themselves." We can't deny the difficulty inherent in many circumstances, nor the pain that accompanies losses. We can, however, choose to see our experiences, no matter how traumatic, as lessons moving us closer to the enlightened state God intends for us.

I will see my experiences as positive lessons today. No one can change my perception but me.

Gratitude enhances all blessings.

Sometimes we just don't feel grateful. We struggle to get out of bed. Begrudgingly, we go to work. Smiling at other people is an effort we can barely make. It's hard to imagine we ever felt grateful or enthusiastic about our lives.

How do we break loose from a negative state of mind? First, we need to remember that whatever we harbor in the mind is what we put there. And with concentrated effort we can be rid of it. Second, making a list of all the blessings we can see in our lives, at this moment, will assure us of God's love. Sometimes we forget that we are here purposefully. And when that happens, it is so easy to lose our enthusiasm. That's normal, so let's not fret for long about it. Instead, let's recapture the proper frame of mind once again by remembering we have a purpose and counting our blessings.

No matter how uninspired I feel, I will remember that God has a plan for me and has blessed me. This will free me from the doldrums.

Most of us became skilled at managing, or at least trying to manage, the lives of many people. We assumed the responsibilities of family members far too often. We were intent on fulfilling very high expectations of ourselves too. So hearing others talk about their struggle with taking full <u>responsibility</u> for their lives didn't register at first. Surely we were already doing that.

We all have to learn what it means to take full responsibility for ourselves.

Fortunately, there is no timetable for how quickly we need to learn the subtleties of this program. Going to meetings frequently, listening to the wisdom of other people, and praying for understanding will help us absorb what there is to learn. We learn, soon enough, that being fully responsible means being responsible for every action we take, every word we speak. It means giving up our manipulative attempts to control and admitting it when we do attempt to control anyway!

Taking responsibility for ourselves is a bigger challenge than we first thought. In time we see it keeps us busy, too busy to mind the business of others.

I can't blame anyone else for what is happening in my life. Today will be as productive and serene as my actions and thoughts dictate.

Keeping track of the shortcomings of other people is second nature to us. Many of us have been obsessed, in fact, with how others live their lives. Since we're all different, it goes without saying that we behave differently, we think differently, and we perform our jobs differently. What's more, our values, even when similar, manifest always in slightly different ways. Thus we have multiple opportunities for judging others.

Acknowledging our defects is the first step in giving them up.

But this program is about keeping the attention on us, instead. It's our behavior, our character defects, and our lives that we have some control over. We have caused problems for ourselves many times, because we haven't been as willing to see our own defects as we have been to see the defects of others. There is no time like the present for changing our focus.

I will keep my eyes on myself today. I realize I am not without defects. But I can change mine.

Honestly reflecting on our past convinces us that most situations we worried ourselves sick over didn't turn out as badly as we had imagined. Or if they did, our Higher Power helped us get through them. Generally, we worry about what we anticipate might happen tomorrow or next month. Our focus is seldom on this day.

Living one day at a time simplifies our lives.

SLIPS

If we could develop the willingness to live just the twenty-four hours before us, we'd hardly ever worry. However, we go through each day almost oblivious to its events. Our minds are somewhere else. Bringing them back to now benefits us in many ways. We can appreciate the sacredness of each interaction that God has given us; we can marvel at the beauty of life surrounding us. We can glean our experiences for God's special messages; we can feel how special our lives are in the grand plan designed by the Creator. None of this can we appreciate if we are not here, now.

Today is it. I can't be sure of tomorrow or next year. Thus I will keep my focus on the treasures God gives me today. They are meant for my special journey.

*Having
principles
to live by
eliminates
guesswork.*

PRACTICING
THE
PRINCIPLES

Newcomers to Twelve Step programs often want to reform the world. And it's easy to understand why. The principles that are offered as guidelines for saner living, if followed by every person alive, would change the complexion of the entire human community.

Many of us came to the program with few, if any, substantive values. We likely felt as if we were missing some key ingredient. Now we are beginning to acquire the same values as the ones that apparently work well for the men and women we are getting to know. This gives us hope for a happier life.

Honest reflection helps us acknowledge that in many situations we simply did the quickest thing or imitated what we saw someone else do. Not feeling very good about anything we did was common, but natural, we thought. How different our lives are now. Seldom do we experience shame over what we say or do. Seldom do we even have to wonder what is the right thing to do.

I can use what I'm learning in the program to help guide my every waking moment today. I'll never be at a loss over what to do. There is always a right way to act, to speak, to think, to care.

JULY

Not letting other people know what's troubling us causes the problem to trouble us even more. "Secrets keep us stuck," say the wise ones on our journey.

Sharing what's on our minds with a friend or sponsor gives that person an opportunity to help us develop a better perspective. On the other hand, staying isolated with our worries exaggerates them.

Staying isolated with our joys isn't helpful either. It minimizes them, thus cheating us out of feeling their full thrill. We deserve joy in our lives—lots of it—because we will have our full measure of pain. Perhaps we fear others will criticize us for being braggarts if we sing forth our joy. But our real friends will sing right along with us. Our joys are deserved; they offset our trials. Telling others about both will let all our experiences count for something.

Sharing our experiences heightens our joy and lessens our pain.

SHARING EMOTIONS

I will remain open to my friends today, sharing both my worries and my joys.

*The people in
Twelve Step
programs are
anonymous.*

Anonymity in a Twelve Step program may not be important to everyone, but to many of us it is crucial. Fortunately, we are assured from our very first meeting that our presence will not be disclosed to anyone outside the meeting. This is why we share first names only.

We have come to a program because we are caught in the web of addiction. Many of us have been living with an active alcoholic or addict for many years. Others of us are alone now, the addict gone but not forgotten. A few of us are fortunate, indeed, for our loved ones are in recovery too.

All of us have come to believe that the Twelve Step program is a lifetime program. We have a reprieve from the "illness" a day at a time, just as long as we use the principles of the Twelve Steps. It may seem strange, at first, to think we'll need this program forever. Surely, we think, not us. But we note, soon enough, the joy and serenity evident in the words and the faces of the old-timers, and then we understand.

I'll keep getting help and hope from a recovery program just as long as I continue to use it. Keeping the membership confidential is one of the first helpful things I can do.

Believing that we can be loved regardless of our defects is not easy. Most of us didn't experience that kind of love as children. What's more, the God we grew up with may have been shaming. Now that we are adults, the criticism we've received from employers, friends, spouses, and other people reinforces our doubt. When our new program friends tell us that our Higher Power loves us unconditionally, we think they are being unrealistic. We can't even love ourselves!

We can accept unconditional love.

Let's give ourselves time to change what we believe and who we believe. Our program will help us. If relied on, the slogans and the Steps will give us a new perspective on every experience. Coming to believe that a Higher Power can wholly love us is a gift of recovery. Then we can begin loving ourselves a little too. Next we'll even begin to love others.

I will believe in unconditional love if I let this program work in my life today.

Before recovery we only wanted to learn how to keep a loved one or friend from drinking or using drugs. That's really all we wanted from the Twelve Step program. How different our lives would be, we thought, if only that person would change.

Personal recovery doesn't mean getting the alcoholic sober.

FREEDOM

Had the program been able to give us what we thought we wanted, we'd be far less content now. What we have learned since entering these rooms is that our own attitudes and behaviors are the real culprits. And we are discovering the tools for taking charge of them.

Our happiness is not dependent on what anyone else does. We didn't understand that before. Now we do. Now we are free from the turmoil we let others stir up in our lives. Now we are free.

I will use my program to help me be free today.

When someone else's behavior triggers an outburst from us, we have relinquished control of ourselves. And we suffer the consequences.

Behaving irrationally is a decision.

It isn't easy to refrain from yelling at loved ones who constantly let us down. Whether it's their drinking or using other drugs or their all-too-common irresponsible behavior, we have expectations for our own lives, and we want others to live up to those expectations! But just as soon as we give in to our anger, we have also reneged on our standards.

It comes down to this: We can be responsible only for ourselves. We can be certain only of our own behavior. Still, that's quite a lot. It means we can be happy regardless of what's happening around us. It means we'll know peace in spite of the chaos in a loved one's life. It means we'll not be ashamed because we yelled when we should have been still.

I will be alert to my opportunities for peaceful decisions today.

Giving our lives and wills to God is a big step.

Chemical dependency has affected each of us in thousands of ways. Undoubtedly, we made excuses for the drinker. Maybe we drank too much too, to keep up. And we were often swallowed by our self-pity. But most of all, we tried to control—the drinker, the drinker's behavior, and the outcome of every situation.

Taking Step Three may scare us at first. It says we want to change. We are ready to give up control. We are willing to let God be in charge—not just of other people, but of us too!

Our fear comes from thinking that God may want us to do something that we hadn't planned on doing. That may be true. However, we'll learn from our friends in the program that we can feel confident we'll never be asked to tackle a goal that we won't be able to handle. We'll always have God's help. Our assignment now is to believe that.

Taking the Third Step each day will help me live through every experience. God is my caring guide today.

We can have freedom from <u>fear</u>. All we have to do is accept our Higher Power as our daily companion. This may sound simple, but many of us, instead of relying on God, have been adamantly self-reliant. It's hard to break this habit. We may also struggle with the possibility that God won't do things our way.

God is our partner.

We are learning from our program friends that when life isn't unfolding as we had anticipated, it's because God has other plans. Getting used to this idea will make fear a rare emotion. And we'll have much more time to enjoy the pleasures of life.

Fear won't trouble me today if I remember that God is my companion.

Taking too much responsibility for other people is irresponsible on our part.

Irresponsibility is a defect few of us think we have. But the truth is, we are being irresponsible when we take on the responsibilities of others! That's a trait many of us honed to near perfection. We may hate to hear this, but it was—and still is—our need to control everyone around us that inspired us to take on others' responsibilities. Accepting that each of us has a unique journey to make, complete with responsibilities suited to our growth, is part of recovery.

Letting others be responsible for themselves is loving and respectful. It's also a big change for us. The support and frequent reminders of program friends keep our attention on our responsibilities. We all want the people around us to be healthier. We want to be healthier too. The first step toward healthier living is letting go, letting them do what needs to be done by them!

I will focus on my life today. I'll let my friends take care of their lives.

Where are we going? What's the plan for our lives? Most of us didn't intend to end up as we have, but here we are! And a significant number of us might not be alive if it weren't for this program. We may have thought we knew where we were headed in our youth, but few of us got there. What we are learning now is that we have an assigned journey and that a Higher Power is in charge. This means we can relax. We don't have to figure anything out. We need only follow our conscience.

We merely need to follow our conscience.

Following our conscience means never intentionally hurting another person. It means following through on the responsibilities that are clearly ours. It means honoring God by being grateful for our many blessings. It means feeling joy for the gift of life we've been given. It means trusting that our journey is special and necessary to the other travelers on our path.

I will remember to appreciate the nudging from my conscience today.

We can be detached and compassionate at the same time.

DETACHEMENT

Being too involved in other people's lives was a common malady before we got into recovery. We considered it a reflection on us personally when children acted out and spouses slipped. We thought that if only we'd been more responsive to their needs, perhaps they wouldn't have failed. But our taking responsibility for their problems released them from the growth they deserved, and no one was helped.

Loving someone doesn't mean we must take away that person's pain. In fact, that may be the most unloving thing we can do. Each of us has a mission, and learning how to handle rough situations is a normal part of our journey. Not letting a loved one grow through his or her painful experiences steals the joy that accompanies having survived and learned from difficulties.

Letting our friends and loved ones suffer the pain of growth is showing compassion in its purest form.

I can love others without trying to solve their problems. Today I'll keep my focus on my own experiences, not those of my loved ones.

Step Eleven suggests that we'll improve our conscious contact with God if we pray and meditate. The meditation part is particularly important. It's the avenue between us and our Higher Power's guidance. Quieting our minds of our obsession with what other people are doing isn't always easy. But it's there, in the quiet, that we'll feel God's guidance, God's message, God's comfort.

If we think too much, we hinder our understanding and our progress.

Having busy minds isn't unusual. Nor is it accidental. Our minds are full because we fill them. If we want quiet minds in order to know God better, we must empty them.

God answers our prayers in the quiet spaces of our minds. Let's listen.

I will clear my mind today so God can reach me with what I need to know.

When we first hear that we have to *give it away,* we are confused. What is it? And to whom do we give it? But listening to the men and women in Twelve Step programs clarifies many things for us. We teach each other the principles for easier living. We learn that by sharing our own experience of strength and hope, we make another's journey easier. Even more importantly, we come to realize that what we share with others is oftentimes what we need a reminder of as well.

We find strength and hope when we share them.

SHARING

The program works and we all get better because of our willingness to listen to and share with others. Isolation no longer appeals to us. The joy we feel at not being alone with our troubles helps us *give it away* and receive it too.

I will look for an opportunity to share with a friend or even a stranger today. We will both get the help we need!

We come into this program hopeless, some of us wretchedly hopeless. But before we leave our very first meeting we experience the thrill of hope, and it almost takes our breath away. It comes through the stories of the group members: We see it in their faces, their smiles. We hear it in their easy laughter. Hope has changed them. We understand before leaving their presence that hope will change us too.

Recovery gives us hope.

Through working this program we discover that having hope makes every situation tolerable. Maybe the drinker will always drink, the cokehead will always use cocaine, and the rebellious youngster will always be in trouble, but we can have a hopeful, spirit-filled attitude anyway. How we feel is never dependent on what someone else does.

I am surrounded by friends who can offer me hope today. If I wake up without it, I'll call someone who can help me find it again.

Giving up a defect can <u>change</u> our lives.

DEFECTS of CHARACTER

We grow fond of some behaviors, even when they cause us harm. No one reacts favorably when we try to be in control, but we do it anyway. Being constantly critical of everyone around us creates much unnecessary friction, but we do that anyway too. It's not that we don't desire more peace in our lives, but that we have gotten stuck in certain behaviors out of habit, and we don't know how else to act, so we do them anyway.

Having a sponsor who lives a good program can open our eyes to behavior worth emulating. Choosing one of his or her healthy habits to substitute for one of our unhealthy ones is a beginning. Seeking God's help in making the substitution will open the door to new opportunities.

What we draw into our lives depends on what we give out. When we change the flavor of what we give, we'll likewise change the flavor of what we receive. Our journey absolutely has to change when we change who we have decided to be.

Today I am embarking on an adventure that I am very much in control of through my behavior. With God's assistance, I can be as helpful and compassionate as the people I admire.

It often seems ludicrous to believe that every situation involving us is by design. For instance, how could we have chosen to experience so closely and personally the disease of addiction? And why were we attracted to lovers who repeatedly abused us emotionally, if not physically? Lots of us absolutely intended to be good parents. So why did our children become substance abusers?

A lesson exists in everything we experience.

There are no adequate answers to these questions. We simply have to trust that what comes our way is meant for our ultimate good. Hindsight provides acceptance, if not always understanding.

Old-timers in this Twelve Step program tell us we are in the right place at the right time. It may sound crazy, but those whom we perceive wise seem to believe it. With time and experience, we'll come to trust their wisdom. We'll also come to value the lessons gained through today's experiences.

I will not fret over whatever is happening today; instead, I'll trust that today's circumstances will make me a wiser person.

Reacting to someone else's behavior gives that person power over us.

PERSONAL POWER

There are thousands of situations and even more people we have no control over. A friend's outburst of anger, a motorist's failure to see our car in a busy intersection, a spouse's relapse—all of these things may upset us. But that upset can be brief if we keep the power over our feelings. Letting someone else decide who we will be, how we will act, and what we will feel implies that we have given up our own life in exchange for whatever someone else wants us to be.

It is not always easy to refrain from reacting to someone, but no one has control over us unless we give it to that person. Even though rude clerks, demanding friends, and naughty children get under our skin easily, we don't have to nurture the irritation. We can take back our power and deliberately decide what our next word, our next action, will be.

I will not let someone else's behavior take charge of my life today.

Do we really gain anything when we sit in judgment of someone else? Perhaps for a moment we feel superior, but through this fellowship we are coming to understand that part of *our* problem is that need to feel superior. Shame for our judgments soon replaces the superior feeling, and we find ourselves lower in spirit and self-esteem than before.

Passing judgment on someone else is self-defeating.

Judging others may have become a habit. Or it may seem to just happen. Regardless of how it happens, it's a pattern of thinking that we *can* control. Acting as if we are not judgmental may be the best tool we can use at first. Then we can replace every judgmental thought with a spoken expression of love, and we will make real progress.

SUPERIORITY

Feeling better about ourselves has always been our goal. At last we are discovering the tools that can help us attain that goal.

I will share love with others today, and I'll feel better for it. They probably will too.

*Seldom
will we
remember
next week
what
bothers us
so much
today.*

We'll have many opportunities to worry before this day ends. Some situations may even be grave. Perhaps a child gets picked up on a drunk-driving charge or a spouse loses another job because of absenteeism. It's not easy to shrug our shoulders when our loved one's troubles infringe on our lives. But the program will help us, and we'll come to understand that shrugging our shoulders doesn't mean we don't care. Rather, it means we are choosing not to do for other people what they must do for themselves.

Life is a process that includes problems that can't always be easily resolved. How refreshing to learn that we don't have to resolve every conflict. We can simply let conflicts be and focus on peaceful images and think loving thoughts instead. We can be certain that we won't remember most of today's troubles tomorrow unless we want to.

Because I used to worry far too much, life wasn't as fun as I'm now capable of making it. Today won't be a repeat of the old days. No matter what happens, I need not worry. God will take care of me.

Letting go of the people in our lives is far more difficult than most of us imagine. We have been so preoccupied with their behavior that it's hard to get them off our minds. Developing a trust in our Higher Power and accepting that each person has a Higher Power can help us let go. But we don't perfect the skill overnight.

Having faith means letting go.

Listening to our friends in Twelve Step meetings, particularly to their examples about letting go, will give us insight and hope. Thus there is no reason why we can't meet with success. Our desire to let go, coupled with faith that God will handle others for us, will make the difference in our behavior. It is often said that anything worth having requires hard work. Learning to let go is no exception.

I know my Higher Power is with me today and every day. I need to remember the same is true for all my friends too. I can have faith and let go.

Listening to a caring friend is one of the ways we hear God's message.

We think we listen, probably because we are in conversation with other people so often. But our own ongoing inner dialogue often shuts out much of what someone is saying. Whether at Twelve Step meetings or at lunch with a friend, we're preoccupied with the many people in our lives, or maybe our jobs, or an event we are organizing. Our minds get filled with the clutter of other times, other places, and we fail to hear the message at *this* single moment.

Peace will come to us when we slow down and quietly listen. When we remember that our friends are often the channel God relies on to reach us, we are eager to hear their words. Since seeking recovery, we have also become seekers of God's will. We may hear our next direction in a friend's suggestion today.

I will quietly listen to the loving words of my friends today.

Is it our nature to be impulsive? Or are we so controlling that we take charge of situations just to keep other people from doing so? Whatever the reason, we often act before we think and thus cause conflicts unnecessarily.

It's not that we never think. In fact, our obsessive thinking about how others should live their lives, all the possible problems we might have before we die, our own failings, may consume many precious hours daily. Our minds are active most of the time. However, our minds need to be still occasionally in order to carefully think through a situation before taking action. And that's what we are striving to master.

The program can help us. Simply remembering that we have a Higher Power who wants to guide our actions and words gives us reason to stop momentarily and let the right thoughts surface. Like anything, slowing down enough to think (or hear and feel) what the best action might be takes practice.

Thinking before acting is harder than it sounds.

IMPULSIVITY

I have learned many things since coming to the program. I now know I have a Higher Power watching over me. I know I have friends who care. I know I am capable of thinking before acting.

Good guidance comes from the right source.

Many times we have been anxious over what to do. In our youth we often followed the direction of friends. That often exaggerated our problems. As adults we looked to our peers too, but until we found our new circle of friends, we often failed to get guidance that lovingly addressed our circumstances.

It's a treasured gift of our program to have a Higher Power who is always there with the guidance we need. But if we still feel uncertain of that guidance, we can turn to trusted friends who will share with us God's wisdom in another way.

The anxiety that troubled us for so long seldom surfaces anymore. What a miracle that is! We thought we'd feel the tightness and the burning and the nausea for our whole life. Now when we get a twinge of it, we know the time has come to go within and ask God for the help we need.

I will get the direction, the comfort, or the answers I really need today if I ask for them from the right source. My Higher Power or my friends in the program can show me the way through my feelings.

It's difficult for some of us to grasp that, as Step One of Alcoholics Anonymous tells us, our lives were unmanageable. We thought we were perfectly organized and efficient. Even so, our inner spaces were always cluttered with the details and problems of other people. Thus our personal lives were not well managed.

"We admitted that our lives had become unmanageable."

A goal we are seeking now through this program is serenity. We get glimpses of it every time we free our minds from tending someone else's business. The very act of managing, or trying to manage, so many other lives made our lives unmanageable. Even though this is difficult to grasp initially, once we understand it, we'll never want to trade in the old behavior for our newly discovered serenity.

Throughout this day I'll ask myself if what I'm about to do is really my concern. If the answer is no, I'll put my attention on God instead.

Self-pity is detrimental and very seductive.

Chemical dependency is a disease that affects every one of us involved with the addict or alcoholic. Because our focus is on the addict or alcoholic, we develop patterns of reacting. For example, we often allow our feelings to be hurt because we take the others' behavior personally rather than seeing it as symptomatic of chemical dependency. Sometimes when our feelings are hurt we get sympathy from others. Even the alcoholic responds to our sadness occasionally. These payoffs, though meager, attract us again and again.

The problem with self-pity is that it changes nothing. It does not stop loved ones from drinking or using drugs. They will do what they will do. *Our* response is the only change we can count on. Refusing to fall into the trap of self-pity will help us dramatically. We will be set free in ways we never imagined. Our lives will take on new meaning when we refuse to be entrapped by self-pity.

I will not feel sorry for myself today regardless of what happens. Joy is far more fun.

We instinctively know which people we have harmed in our lives. Is anything to be gained from writing down their names? At first we probably think not. After all, we haven't forgotten them. But a good sponsor will tell us that listing the names readies us for the opportunity to make amends. And until we have made them, our relationships suffer not only with the people we have harmed but also with everyone else.

Do we really need to make a list of those we have harmed?

The unfinished business in our lives keeps us from the growth we deserve. We came to a recovery program because we wanted help, and the founders of Alcoholics Anonymous, in writing down the Twelve Steps, defined the methods by which we get it. Following the Steps ensures that we'll change in the ways we want to. Doing the Eighth Step, as written, is a must.

Our opportunity to make amends will come just as quickly as we become entirely ready to make them. The happiness we desire in all our relationships can follow only when we have done our work.

I am here because I want a better life. I'll do what I need to today to open the door to it.

Hopelessness can be replaced with peacefulness.

The very first meeting of Al-Anon or other Twelve Step programs cultivates a significant change in most people. We no longer feel that our lives are hopeless. Our problems haven't miraculously disappeared, but we sense from the others in the group that we'll survive them.

A crucial benefit of the program is the number of available meetings. Any day we feel worried or on the fringe of hopelessness once again, we can go to a meeting and our hopeful perspective will return. The stories and the support of others who really know how we feel make it possible for us to continue our journey.

The tools we in the program learn to use contribute to the sense of hope we now feel too. In the past our hopelessness about our condition overwhelmed us. Now we hear and see how the tools have worked for others. Turning to a Higher Power for solace and guidance is one of the first tools for change that we can learn to use.

I will feel peace and hope today in proportion to my commitment to using the tools of the program.

Blessings abound in our lives. Even when all we can see is the havoc the alcoholic has caused, we need to remember the tiny joys: the call from a friend, the smiles from strangers, the beauty of nature. It's so easy to fall into hopelessness when we focus all our attention on what the addict is doing despite our pleas.

Remember the smallest blessings.

We can cultivate a brighter outlook in much the same way we cultivate a garden. We can plant the seed of God's love in our minds every morning and water it throughout the day with tiny prayers of gratitude. If we do this, our hearts will be uplifted by nightfall. Making a practice of this will change us completely.

It may sound too simple at first, but the winners among us have learned how to feel happy even in the midst of conflict. They aren't privileged in any special way. We can have what they have with a little "gardening."

I deserve to feel good about my life today. I have many blessings that I take for granted. I'll think about them today, and my attitude will reflect my gratitude.

The busyness of our lives keeps us believing that we are in control, that we are managing just fine. And no doubt there are some things we are handling: Meals are cooked. We haven't missed many days of work. We're on top of the bills too, maybe. But we aren't peaceful. What's wrong?

". . . our lives had become unmanageable."

For many of us, our incessant thinking, running, doing, is what's wrong. We are on a treadmill of activity that passes for *good management.* We are desperate to show other people that we are *just fine.* In reality, we are being managed by our obsession to stay busy. If we are busy, our lives don't seem so close to falling apart.

What a gift this program is offering us! We can get off the treadmill. We can slow our thoughts to a more natural pace. We can prioritize the things we must do today. We can follow the example of others who understand our obsession.

I will quietly *go about my life today. Doing one thing peacefully is enough to accomplish.*

What drives us to complicate our lives? Some people would say our compulsion to control. It's true we want to take charge of most situations, particularly if they involve us or other people we care about. We worry when others are in charge, fearful they won't have our interests uppermost in mind. What we need to remember is that God's interests need serving, and letting go of situations so that God can have full charge of the outcomes will ensure we'll get whatever we need.

Keep it simple.

Attending only to ourselves makes each twenty-four-hour block so much more manageable. What might happen tomorrow need not concern us today; God will help us when the time has come. What might transpire next year is way down on God's list too. The experiences we need will occur at their own proper time and with God as director.

Today we can do the Third Step, and God will take care of the rest. Life can be a lot simpler than we make it.

I will keep it simple today and do only what I need to do. I won't try to live anyone else's life. I'll work with my Higher Power to live only my own.

Forgiveness allows more love in our lives.

Painful memories from childhood and adulthood can linger. Hearing sponsors and people at meetings say we need to forgive those transgressions disturbs us initially. Shouldn't those who hurt us be made to suffer too?

The wise ones in our meetings help us understand that holding on to anger and resentments injures us far more than the people who originally hurt us. Eventually we realize that hanging on to injustices jeopardizes our relationships. That's not to say the injustices didn't happen, only that keeping them alive in our minds and hearts keeps us from knowing and feeling the healing grace of God's love. Forgiveness will someday lead to love for all people, past and present, in our lives. We never have to accept what they did as okay, but we have to let the memory die before we can heal.

I contribute to my healing today by forgiving those who may have hurt me. By letting go of my pain I will begin to feel more of God's love.

Choosing silence rather than injuring someone with our words fills us with hope that we
can change. For much of our past we had let
our impulses lead us, and this hurt many people who were close to us. Often we meant
well. We honestly thought our way of living
was the best. We never really understood
when we were in confrontation that each person's perspective was valid.

*Compliment
rather than
criticize.*

It's not easy to quit judging others. It almost seems that our minds do it automatically, but, of course, we have trained them.
We can stop being critics when we use our
minds to notice only the good qualities of
others. We'll discover that the content of
what we say changes too.

We feel so much better when we compliment rather than criticize. It empowers us to
know that we can change negative behavior.
It also helps those close to us. Their good
qualities are enhanced every time we acknowledge them.

*I can change me today. I will be complimentary
or, at least, I will say nothing. That might help
a loved one change too.*

AUGUST

Coming to believe that a Higher Power can help us and relieve us of our worry may take time if we have spent years trying to stop someone's drinking or worrying about how to keep the family together. From others in this program we can learn the steps to take. Becoming willing to pray is the first one.

When it seems we have no recourse, we can always pray.

We'll soon discover that the power of prayer is awesome. Here are six compelling reasons why: (1) Prayer promises relief when we are anxious. (2) Prayer connects us with our Higher Power when we feel isolated and full of fear. (3) Prayer frees our minds from the obsession to plan other people's lives. (4) Prayer helps us take action when we feel compelled to change the circumstances of our lives. (5) Prayer becomes a wonderful resource to draw on when living through our painful moments. (6) And prayer gives us the willingness to accept God's solution for every problem that plagues us.

I will utilize prayer today every time I wonder what I should do.

Other people's perspectives are valid.

RESPECT

RESTRAINT

T² THINK
BEFORE
SPEAKING

Many of us have believed our opinions on all matters are right. This has put us at odds with family, friends, and strangers. Accepting that every person's perspective is valid, at least for that person, may seem out of the question at first. But after growing accustomed to the idea, we will find great relief, knowing that we don't have to be in conflict anymore. We are so much freer when we respect others' opinions.

The best way to remember that others have valid perspectives is by developing the habit of momentarily pausing before responding to another's words or actions. We will get good at letting others "be." And *we* will feel so much better for it.

I will momentarily pause before responding to others today. This will save me from lots of tension.

Nobody has the perfect spouse, job, car, home, clothes, or body. We simply have what we have. It's what we do with what we have that makes the difference. We can take charge of how we think and be grateful for our blessings, making the most of them, or we can sulk and wallow in self-pity because we got shortchanged in some aspect of our lives.

We will never benefit from martyrdom.

Playing the martyr has a payback, though a limited one. From some people, we'll get the sympathy we think we deserve. We'll feel understood and released from the high expectations we feared they'd have of us. We'll figure we can slide by, doing very little at home or on the job. But we won't be well served by this.

Those who support our martyrdom hurt us. We won't find those kinds of people in Al-Anon or other Twelve Step circles. Instead, we'll meet men and women who will challenge us to take charge of our actions, our attitudes, our responsibilities. And the more we assert ourselves, the less we'll experience the self-pity that used to swallow us. The real prize worth coveting is empowerment. That is guaranteed if we work a good program.

I will feel the personal power I deserve if I put my recovery principles to the test today.

Giving with no strings attached is true giving.

The disease of chemical dependency is reflected in myriad ways. As we've learned, the entire family is affected. We have sought recovery because our behavior causes us problems too. Getting well might be even more difficult for us than for alcoholics or other addicts. Their first step is to give up alcohol or other drugs; ours is to stop most of the behaviors we've perfected over the years, behaviors we developed to control and manipulate others.

Giving is one such behavior. Of itself, giving is a very worthy characteristic. However, most of us have used giving as a not so subtle way to control. Too often it worked, at least in the short run, and giving became a tool to get what we wanted. Recovery can help us practice true giving. We might not get from others what we'd like, but we will feel rewarded just the same. Giving up manipulation gives us back our self-worth.

I will check my motives before giving anything today. If I hope to get something in return, I'll begin again.

We all know people who seem to court disaster. They are frequently in conflict with other people. They get little joy from life. They are critical of most experiences and not happy about most people. Perhaps we are sometimes like these people ourselves.

A bad ~~attitude~~ makes for a bad life.

It's easier to see how others' attitudes affect their lives than it is to recognize how our attitudes affect our lives. But attitude, for all of us, is profoundly influential. We will experience each situation according to the attitude we cultivate. Even though it *feels* as if our attitude simply happens, we orchestrate it. And we can change it. A tiny decision is all that's necessary.

Our lives mirror our attitudes. Our friends who seem more blessed than we are probably nurture that attitude.

I will focus on my attitude today. How I think will be reflected in what I experience.

Believing in a Higher Power changes everything.

Faith in a Higher Power doesn't come easily for many people, particularly those for whom the past has been painful. Acting as if there is a God is the best many people can do at first. And that's good enough.

What's to be gained from believing in a Higher Power? Peace of mind comes first. Knowing that we're not alone, that we have a companion to share every burden with, makes any struggle easier to handle.

But belief doesn't mean that we'll no longer have problems, that we'll be guaranteed happiness. Life is ebb and flow, good and bad, up and down. Nothing has to destroy us, though, and that's where our faith comes in. With our knowledge that God is present always, we can move through troubling experiences, confident that we'll survive—confident, in fact, that we'll grow from the experience.

With my Higher Power's help, I will get hope and relief today in all my experiences, no matter how troubling.

Many of us come into the program certain we were the victims, not the perpetrators, of harm. We often bore the brunt of the chemically dependent person's rage and insanity. But the program teaches us that we too behaved in harmful ways. Our "raging" silence was harmful at times; so was our disgust. Neither our excuses for an alcoholic's behavior nor our attempts to shame someone into changing helped. We are not innocent of all charges. We too have amends to make.

Once we understand our own past transgressions, we can say we're sorry. And that's a beginning. But admitting we were wrong and then quite deliberately changing how we behave is what making amends is all about. Initially our payoff is that we can feel intimate with other people again, and even more important, we get practice in changing who we are. We get to become who we want to be.

Making amends is not just being sorry.

T²
STEP 9
+
STEP 10

I will make the amends that are mine to make today. I will feel good about my every effort.

*Sharing
our lessons
reinforces
our
growth.*

TELLING
OUR STORIES

T2
SPONSORSHIP

Many people benefit when we share our experiences, and we are at the top of the list. The founders of this program were wise. They knew that the greatest value of sharing one's experience, strength, and hope was that the storyteller was strengthened and inspired by each telling.

Every one of us, no matter how dedicated we are to working the program and using its tools, gets off center occasionally. Perhaps we momentarily forget the importance of humility and rely on ourselves rather than God for direction. It doesn't take long for our lives to feel out of control once that happens.

Helping someone else at the very time we feel unbalanced mysteriously guides us back to our own center. It's almost as though our Higher Power is reaching us through the words we share with someone who is struggling. The result is clarity for both of us.

I will honor the contact a sponsee or friend makes with me today. Every contact is for a purpose.

Detachment is difficult to understand, particularly for those of us used to minding everyone else's business. In the old days taking care of people, protecting their feelings and cleaning up their messes (real or imaginary), was how we showed our love. Our self-worth came from taking care of others. Our victory was hollow, but we didn't know how to live differently.

Detachment helps us love others and ourselves.

The fellowship is teaching us that detachment is *real* love, a *real* victory. At first it sounds cold and unloving to turn away from loved ones who are in obvious pain. However, this ultimately makes us take responsibility for our own lives. The greatest gift we can give others is the freedom to live their own lives, make their own mistakes, discover their own "way" to a more serene life. The miracle is that we'll find a more serene life too.

God, help me mind my own business today. Letting my loved ones alone is the best help I can give them.

Feeling superior harms us.

+2 OR INFERIOR

SUPERIORITY +2 INFERIORITY

We all have unique talents. Astronauts, painters, teachers, and great athletes are no more valuable in God's eyes than we are. We share the stage of life equally. But we often forget this. And when we do, we begin to feel either inferior or superior to the other people on our path. In those moments, our talent is overshadowed by our feelings. We aren't at peace with ourselves or others.

Our relationships grow and change through the talent we each bring to them. It is not coincidental that certain people are drawn together to fulfill one another's destiny. Feeling either superior or inferior disregards the divinity of each of us. Instead, we must do whatever it takes to believe in our equality with others. Our program offers us a wonderful dress rehearsal.

If I'm feeling superior OR INFERIOR today, I'll ask my Higher Power for help in noticing everyone's talents.

Asking our Higher Power what to do in a certain situation always provides us with a response. We feel so much saner when the torment of anxiety isn't shadowing us.

The first time we read the <u>Eleventh Step</u> we didn't understand how it would change our lives. Prayer wasn't familiar to many of us, so we weren't accustomed to listening for God's reply. Now we know there is always a reply: Our task is to quietly wait for it.

What freedom we feel, now that we don't have to figure out every detail of our lives. If we wonder how to handle our relationships with difficult people, God will show us. When a loved one gets into trouble, God will help us let that person solve the problem. On those days when we feel afraid and don't know why, we can remember God's presence and gain courage and comfort.

Nothing in our lives feels the same, now that we have conscious contact with our Higher Power. And how lucky for us that it's available every minute of the day.

Conscious contact means closeness with our Higher Power.

My Higher Power is as close as my willingness to think of the spirit within me. I won't be worried about any experience today if I use my mind to my advantage.

Meetings are one way of carrying the message.

Step Twelve reminds us that part of our responsibility as recovering people is to carry the message to others who still suffer. That doesn't mean we have to reveal our stories to strangers. Nor do we have to break our anonymity if we think it might jeopardize us or members of our family. But when we are at meetings with others who are seeking answers, we are safe to share our personal message of what it was like, what happened, and what it's like now.

Carrying our message of change and hope strengthens our own reliance on this program. We hear the old-timers in the program say we have to "give it away to keep it," but we can't know what that means until we experience the relief and hope that happens each time we honestly share a part of our lives with someone else. The "honeymoon high" that newcomers often experience when they first get involved in the program is repeated again and again, as long as we actively carry our message.

I will help myself by carrying my message of hope today. What I give away will come back to me, many times over.

Anxiously waiting for a certain phone call, dwelling on a cutting criticism, watching for an expected rebuff—these were common behaviors for many of us. Our lives were far too focused on other people. And when they weren't overtly loving us or showing respect, we doubted ourselves, often losing our confidence even in the middle of a task. How others treated us controlled how we thought of ourselves. We seldom considered that others' insecurities caused them to try to diminish us.

How we behave is a reflection of how we think.

Now we are free from their control. We are spending time with people who are seeking a healthier way of life. Using affirmations and strengthening our relationship with our Higher Power are helping us develop healthier attitudes about ourselves. As our self-esteem grows, so will our accomplishments. Not letting others have power over how we'll behave is the ticket to a happier, more successful future. The Twelve Step program is making our independence possible

I won't be controlled by others' responses. With my Higher Power's help I will be successful today. My self-esteem depends on me.

Genuine love accepts, not controls, others.

UNCONDITIONAL LOVE

We claim to do many things for the sake of love. But correcting other people "for their own good" isn't love. Carrying out the responsibilities of a family member isn't love. Lying to protect the feelings of a friend can't be called love. Making amends that hurt someone in order to relieve our own guilt isn't love, either. Learning what love is, is one of our opportunities in the program.

Conditional love was what many of us learned growing up. Because of what we learned at home, however, we often failed in our attempts to truly love others.

Now that we are in the program, the First Step will lead us to a new understanding of love. Admitting we can't control others will open the door to accepting them as they are. For many of us, this admission makes it possible to go one step further—to love them as they are. Our relationships will be much more satisfying when we quit trying to control everything and the resulting stress is removed. Love eases our lives, and the more frequently it is expressed, the greater our satisfaction.

Being willing to love others as they are makes it easier to love myself. Today will be rich and satisfying in proportion to how loving I am toward others.

Step Twelve is specific in its suggestion that we work all the Steps if we expect to be spiritually awake. But what does it mean to be spiritually awake? Few of us know what it means when we first come to a Twelve Step program. We feel defeated, spiritless, probably embarrassed, because we haven't been able to keep the alcoholic from drinking. We have not expected God to participate actively in our lives. Besides, we may reason, surely our lives wouldn't be this bad if God had been present in the first place.

Our spiritual awakening comes from working the Steps.

Our assignment is to work each Step, but first we must develop an understanding of each one. That's hard unless we follow the example of other people, yet when we do, the subtle changes begin to occur quickly in our lives. That inspires us to keep working; the irony is that work, in most instances, means giving up a number of things: our control, our expectations of others, our insistence on certain outcomes, our anger and resentment, our spiteful behavior, our self-pity. The more we give up, the more we will awaken to the knowledge that God will do for us what we have not been able to do.

My spirit will be awakened a bit more each time I ask God to take over for me.

Loving others is directly proportional to how much we love ourselves.

SELF-LOVE

Do we really love ourselves? Do we forgive ourselves when we blatantly judge others or when we fail on the job or in a relationship? Expecting perfection of ourselves is setting a standard that is unachievable. To love means to accept ourselves wholly, failings and all.

We can practice forgiving ourselves and others. Forgiving ourselves for our transgressions, regardless of what they are, will get easier with practice. Forgiving others will remove the barriers that separate us and prevent us from knowing love.

Our Higher Power asks very little of us. Careers aren't dictated. We can live almost anywhere we want. We may choose to have children or remain childless. All that's really asked is that we live our lives with love in our hearts. Being willing to love ourselves helps us love others too.

If I'm feeling hateful or judgmental toward someone today, I'm not loving myself either.

Some of us sharing these meetings mistakenly thought we were supposed to manage everyone and everything. We managed children and spouses, and when we could, neighbors, co-workers, and friends. And we saw our ability to manage other people's lives as proof of our worthiness. Letting others manage themselves, however, is the real asset, and working on its development takes perseverance.

Being a good manager doesn't mean managing someone else's life!

CONTROL

The appeal of managing others is clearly to protect ourselves. When we can't count on them to do what we want, without our input, then we must get involved. Unfortunately, over the years many people let us manage them. Oftentimes their alcoholism or other drug dependence opened the door to us. We took this as a sign that we were needed. Learning now that we are needed, but not to manage others, is a challenging lesson.

I won't manage others' lives today. I can offer suggestions to others, if asked, but I will only manage myself.

*To some,
problems
are really
opportunities.*

OPTIMISM

How we define our experiences determines what use we make of them. Before embarking on this recovery path, many of us struggled through most experiences feeling either angry or hurt. We envisioned people around us as the enemy, which made it difficult to perceive any experience as beneficial.

The program tells us that all experiences are gifts from God. We are members of the human community for a purpose, and the more quickly we turn to our Higher Power for direction, the sooner we'll be able to see that every situation is an opportunity to grow and change and contribute. That's why we're here.

It's good advice to look at the glass not as half-empty but as half-full.

An opportunity that I hadn't counted on will probably come my way today. I will seek my Higher Power's guidance.

How frequently do we compare ourselves to others? Are we sincerely happy for friends who are successful? Are we jealous when attractive people enter a room? Are we crushed when we don't win at games? It's not unusual to feel *less than*, to feel we don't measure up, but it's never necessary. The program will help us change.

Feeling equal to others is far more peaceful.

Believing we are here to fulfill a specific purpose, one that no other person has been assigned, is wonderful food for thought for those of us who struggle with feelings of inadequacy. We begin to understand how very necessary each of us is, and we no longer feel the need to compare ourselves with others. With the *insanity* gone, we become willing to be guided by a Higher Power as we play our particular role.

UNIQUENESS TZ EQUALITY

How much wiser and saner we feel with the Twelve Steps leading us. And feeling equal to others frees us to put our energies toward the task that is our assignment. What inspiration this new understanding gives us.

I am here to do the special work God assigns. No one else has my task. With a gentle mind, trust, and a willing heart, I'll do it well.

We all have "defects of character." Seeing and accepting them are the first steps to changing them.

ACCEPTANCE

A glaring defect of character for many of us is focusing on other people's behavior. We become obsessed with how it affects us. Trying to be the center of everyone's universe becomes habitual, fraught with failure, and dangerously unhealthy. Trying to control *anyone else* is a losing battle.

It's quite a change of perspective to look at only our own behavior. It seems far easier to look at the behavior of others. However, we will feel stuck, helpless, and in time hopeless if we don't get our focus off others and on to what we are doing. It's only ourselves that we can change. And every little change we make will have unexpected results within our relationships. That's the real miracle. Those glaring defects we thought others had will be all but gone when we attend to changing our own.

T² WE FOCUS ON OTHERS RATHER THAN LOOK HONESTLY AT OURSELVES.

I will find greater happiness with other people today if I accept them and try to change only me.

The disease of alcoholism blurs the bound-aries between people. Taking over the alcoholic's responsibilities just seems to happen. Letting the drinker's behavior control how we feel and what we do also just seems to happen. Trying to make drinkers stop abusing chemicals, us, and themselves becomes an obsession. We can't separate ourselves from their craziness, and pretty soon we're crazy too.

Our lives are entwined with the lives of those we love.

It isn't easy to recognize the boundaries between others and ourselves. But the program offers us the help we need. Doing an inventory as suggested in the Fourth Step is a good place to begin, because it will help us recognize who we really are. Until we know that, we can't see how often our actions are in conflict with our values. We're lucky to have the tools for changing how we live. The changes we make may free the alcoholic to change too.

My involvement with anyone else's behavior today needs close monitoring. I can remain fully in charge of who I want to be.

Crises hold powerful lessons.

Living in fear of a crisis controls us mentally and emotionally; we get trapped in negativity, perceiving our experiences as threatening even when they aren't. The expectation of a crisis can even trigger one if we're too focused on negative events.

Sponsors can help us realize that crises don't have to be feared. We'll discover that every stumbling block holds a lesson. When we begin turning to God to see us through every difficult circumstance, we will discover freedom from fear. With the help of this program, we'll soon be able to look on a crisis as a gift of growth from God. We might even relish crises as opportunities.

If my mind begins to move toward fear today, I'll call on my Higher Power and my sponsor for the reminders I need to get my thinking back on track.

We often hear newcomers or our sponsees ask, "How do I know my will isn't God's will?" Experience has shown us they are the same on occasion. Still, the best response is that we have an intuitively peaceful feeling when we are fulfilling God's will. On the other hand, when chaos invades our inner spaces we are probably acting against God's will in favor of our own.

Accepting God's will as our own simplifies life.

We hear from seasoned program people that this is a simple program. However, to most of us it feels very complicated initially. We have spent decades learning to be strong, forceful, exemplary managers, invulnerable to hurt and adversity. Now it's suggested that we turn over to God most of what we've spent our lives trying to master. It's not easy to do. We can't fathom how to go about it. But we can recognize conflict when it's occurring, and that may be the best indication to turn to God for guidance.

If I feel good about what I'm doing or saying, or contemplating doing or saying, then I can be fairly certain that God's will is in charge of mine. Today will go as smoothly as my will allows it to go.

First Things First is a simple slogan we can use to determine our priorities.

There is always a sensible order for handling whatever we need to do today. Obsessing about all our responsibilities at once makes us anxious. No doubt we have all stared at stacks of work or sat at the kitchen table mulling over our "to do" list, immobilized by the quantity of work to be done. Consequently, the first time we hear the slogan First Things First, we wonder how it can be applied to our lives.

We may need to ask a sponsor for help in prioritizing our responsibilities at first. It's not easy to focus on them one at a time. But there is always a natural order to handling our responsibilities. We simply lack the objectivity to see it.

Once we have experienced setting priorities and the relief it gives us from thinking of all our tasks at once, we'll count on the slogan First Things First. It will bring balance to our lives every day.

I need to do many jobs today. To keep productive and sane, I'll use the slogan First Things First.

Many of us are obsessed with trying to control the significant people in our lives. We sit in judgment and feel certain that our understanding of certain situations is more accurate than theirs. And because our tentacles are out, we create resistance, exactly what we had hoped to avoid.

Experiences mirror attitudes.

Why is it so difficult to learn that other people need to be responsible for themselves? We are never successful in our attempts to control, at least in the long run, and our actions or words cause tension, if not outright battles. Conflict becomes a way of life. Nobody wins, everybody loses.

Giving up the "I'm right" attitude is a big undertaking. Without the help of the people and the principles of recovery, we'd not likely be able to do it. Perseverance pays off, however. And the irony is, when we give up our controlling ways, other people sometimes do what we want them to.

My attitude will influence my experiences today. If the day is rocky, I need to look within.

Defining "good" in my life is up to me.

We've heard, "Life is as good as we make it," but this sounds far too simplistic. We look at friends, family, and co-workers and often see much unhappiness. If it's up to us to make life good, why do so few take advantage of the opportunity?

It's not that we don't want happiness. All of us do. But many of us mistakenly think happiness comes from outside ourselves. For example, when other people shower us with love, we're happy. When the boss compliments our work, we're happy. On the other hand, relying on our inner wisdom to tell us we're worthy and believing we are worthy are untapped skills for most of us. Fortunately, we are in the right place to acquire these skills.

Twelve Step programs will teach us if we are ready to take responsibility for our own happiness. Our program friends are learning how to rely on their inner wisdom and their God, and we are learning from their example. It's really only a simple change in perspective. It's looking within, not without, for knowledge of our worth. There's no mystery to it. We can do it just as they are doing it.

I will monitor how I evaluate my experiences today. Living peacefully and happily is up to me.

What does it mean to be right? Does it mean the other person is wrong? Or that the other person simply has given in? Getting our way may be the result of the scrimmage, but what have we really won? Oftentimes we're left feeling guilty or ashamed, having pushed too hard to be the victor.

Having to be right means unending conflict.

Needing to be right may reveal our insecurity. Instead, we can rely on our Higher Power for strength and comfort when we feel inadequate. Relying on that same support during a conflict erases our need to be victorious over the other person. We'll win instead a moment of peace. That will make us the real victor, every day of our lives.

I will thankfully give in if a conflict arises today. My peace of mind is too valuable to argue away.

Listening is a gift to ourselves.

Why is it so hard to really listen? Perhaps one reason is that for decades people have been talking *at* us rather than *with* us. Parents, teachers, friends, bosses, lovers, or spouses have offered us years of accumulated talk. But how much of this talk have we really let in?

Listening is valuable. What the people around us communicate can beckon us to the growth that is necessary to fulfill our purpose here. Even when we don't want to hear what they have to say, their words can trigger insight and new direction for us, and can deepen our understanding of our journey.

Most of us get an occasional glimpse of our purpose in this life, and when it comes we feel radiant, uplifted. But mostly we have to trust that God is showing us the way even if we don't see it. That's where listening to other people helps. They can be the messengers of our Higher Power.

I will remember that God is revealing my purpose through the men and women talking to me today. I will listen.

Getting back into old destructive behavior is far more common than we first thought. Recovery has given us the tools to prevent it, but we're human. Occasionally we resist our better judgment. Instead, we let the chaos of the moment take charge of our thinking. We rant and rave, inflicting harm on whoever is close. In the shame that follows we convince ourselves, at least momentarily, that we'll never lose control again. But of course we will.

"Slips" are not the exclusive domain of alcoholics.

Chemical dependency is an illness. And though we are not obsessed with using alcohol or other drugs, we are obsessed with the behavior of other people. Our resistance to letting them alone pushes us to our limit of personal control. Vigilance regarding our thoughts and actions, coupled with a reliance on a Higher Power for guidance and serenity, will help us escape the seduction of trying to control others.

Slipping will always be a possibility. But the principles of the program, its Steps and slogans, and our sponsors will be available in our time of crisis. The choice to seek help will be our safeguard when we feel a "slide" coming on.

My obsession with others might suck me into chaotic situations, but I can escape with the program's help. I won't slip today.

Sharing our lessons helps us acknowledge our growth.

We need to share what we have learned from working the Twelve Steps and living the principles of the program. Taking stock of how our lives have changed for the better can keep us willing to continue following the Steps. They have *worked* for us. Our sharing makes it possible for newcomers to experience hope for change in their lives too.

The most important element of this program is the interplay between "teacher" and "student." Sharing what has worked makes us teachers by example, even though we are only baby steps away from the role of student ourselves: at one moment, teacher; at the next, student. We are always learning from others, and others are learning from us. The circle of growth continues. That's what recovery programs are all about.

I want to be part of the circle of growth. I'll help someone else by telling what has worked for me. If I need help, I'll listen.

When we are at peace, we laugh easily over the many times we fought against admitting we were wrong. Many of us grew up in homes where <u>mistakes</u> meant punishment. We learned at an early age to cover up for them. It's second nature for us to do so still. However, since discovering Twelve Step recovery, we have become committed to changing that trait.

Being wrong isn't the end of the world.

Being human means being wrong sometimes and making mistakes. The Twelve Step program tells us it's progress, not perfection, we are after. But the past expectations of parents linger in our minds. We feel ashamed and conspicuous when we are wrong, and we assume others evaluate our worth on how often we are right. This is a difficult assumption to discard. Fortunately, excellent teachers and role models surround us in recovery programs.

None of us is mistake-proof. All of us are wrong sometimes. And each of us is capable of learning to laugh at our mistakes. Let's help each other today.

Mistakes are a part of everyone's life. I am no different from my friends in the program. Like everyone else, I too can learn from my mistakes.

SEPTEMBER

How our lives have changed! Even a short time ago we'd not have imagined we would be here, now. We are on the road to recovery, and we are learning that we can handle whatever comes. Our Higher Power will see to it!

We can handle anything one day at a time.

SURVIVAL

Regardless of age, most of us have survived experiences that were traumatic, perhaps even dangerous. We probably didn't look to our Higher Power for strength; we made it through the troubled time because we were survivors. The good news is that we're still survivors and we'll survive whatever comes with greater ease and fewer struggles when we let God direct us twenty-four hours at a time.

I am in good hands. No experience will be more than I can handle.

Taking appropriate action becomes easier with practice.

Whether we *act* or *react* can have a profound impact on our lives. Letting someone's drinking, irritability, or depression take charge of our own feelings and behavior means having a less than satisfactory life at best. And many of us had lives of reactionary desperation before our introduction to this Twelve Step program.

At first we may not understand the difference between *acting* and *reacting*. Perhaps the easiest way to discern the difference is by how we feel. We feel empowered by our carefully selected responses to a situation—by acting. We feel drained, powerless, and oftentimes hopeless by an emotional and irrational response—by reacting.

Fortunately, we can learn to quit reacting. Taking a ten- or fifteen-second pause before making a move will keep us in charge of what we do.

Many times today I'll be on the verge of reacting when I could act instead. I pray to remember to pause.

The longer we avoid making amends, the harder it is, or so it seems. By doing a mini-inventory every evening and owning who we have been all day long, we get in the habit of "seeing" ourselves before the baggage piles up. Admitting our shortcomings immediately also keeps us aware of the progress we've made in changing our behavior.

Prompt amends are easier to make.

It sometimes seems the founders of the Twelve Step program thought of everything. They emphasized that as important as cleaning up the past is, keeping the present free of new messes is even more important. We have been given a second chance for a really good life. Regardless of who we are sharing life with—people who are still actively using or people who are abstinent—our own lives will be what we make of them. Getting into the habit of admitting when we are wrong and asking for forgiveness will make every other part of our journey easier and a closer match to God's will.

I am eager to change. My first task is to recognize at least one thing I need to do differently and to go about doing it today.

Complacency breeds old behavior and unnecessary problems.

"The promises," as suggested in the Big Book, clearly indicate that we have work to do if we want the rewards that are guaranteed in this program of recovery. Getting complacent, not using the tools that the program has taught us, opens the door to backsliding. Before long we are caught in the old game of manipulation; tension fills our lives again.

There are simple antidotes to complacency. Gratitude is one of them. Every morning we can take a few moments to appreciate all the goodness in our lives. Another powerful antidote is taking the time to consciously contact our Higher Power. God is always available to help us; we simply have to open the door. Sharing hope with others is perhaps the most powerful of the antidotes because it helps at least two people—ourselves and the listener who hears our story.

The Twelve Step program has made each of us a messenger for God. When we isolate, forgetting our role in this picture that's unfolding, the old attitudes and behaviors return. We are told to be "painstaking" about our efforts. The benefits will match them.

I will be present to the others in my life today and will acknowledge God in all that I do. My conscientiousness won't allow me to be complacent.

Wringing our hands over circumstances gone awry wastes our energy. In any twenty-four hours we will experience many situations that will evolve according to God's plan, rather than our own. We'd feel our spirits being lifted if we could assume that any ripple in a day's activities is simply God's way of reminding us that outcomes are not ours to orchestrate.

Problems are opportunities for stretching our minds.

OPENNESS

As we grow accustomed to a broader range of perspectives than just our own, we become more aware of the multiplicity of views. This stretches our minds, teaching us to see in new and valuable ways. It is no accident that each of us brings a unique contribution and personal viewpoint to the table. God's design has gathered us together to learn from one another.

I will appreciate other people's viewpoints today. It is part of God's plan for my growth.

Giving up fear is always an option.

For some of us, fear is a constant companion. The hot ball of anxiety in the stomach becomes a way of life, and we never expect to feel any other way. We worry about the well-being of our chemically dependent loved ones, we worry about keeping our jobs, we worry about everyone's health. We worry about worrying too much!

Yet there is another way to live, and we're being introduced to that in recovery. At first, however, it seems impossible to give up worry. What will we do with our minds? For so long we have kept them filled with worries. Learning from sponsors and friends that we can pray for freedom from worry and knowing our Higher Power is working in our lives give us hope that we can change. Many of our Twelve Step friends have given up worry and are sharing their joy with us now. If they can do it, so can we.

T²
WORRY

I will meditate on God's being present with me today. I'll have no worries to hinder my joy.

While growing up, we weren't always given good guidance by friends or even family members. People helped us to the best of their ability, no doubt, but none of them could foresee the future. Everyone's perspective was limited.

God's guidance keeps us on course.

As members of the Twelve Step program, we have a limited personal perspective too, but we are learning to rely on the constant presence and guidance of a Higher Power, which is far different from depending on very fallible human beings who may not rely on spiritual solutions. When we seek help from each other *and* our Higher Power, we can feel fairly confident that the suggestions made have a connection to God's guidance. And we are learning from sponsors and other long-time members that God never gives us a wrong direction.

I can trust the information and guidance I seek if I know the people I turn to are intent on fulfilling God's will in their lives.

SEPTEMBER 8

Have we admitted we are powerless?

Taking the First Step is necessary if we hope to find joy in our lives. Up to now we have been trying to force, manipulate, shame, or even *love* someone into doing things our way. Sometimes we are even successful. But getting other people to do things against their will is bittersweet, at best. And there is never a guarantee that they won't do what they want at the first opportunity.

Accepting that we are powerless over others isn't really as difficult as it sounds. More than anything, it is simply a different way of looking at our experiences. Coming to understand that we aren't responsible for the actions of anybody but ourselves feels like a vacation when appreciated from the right perspective. Being powerless over others is really quite empowering for us personally. The joy we want and deserve will follow.

Accepting my powerlessness over someone else today will give me the relief I deserve.

Nearly every day we ponder what to do about a nagging situation. We review in our minds the "he saids, she saids" until we're worn out, oftentimes still troubled about what to do. And then we remember we have guiding voices all around us.

Wisdom comes wrapped in many packages.

What lucky people we are. If it weren't for the role chemical dependency has played in our lives, we might never have known that a Higher Power was present to help us. Nor would we have known that a passage in a special book held a message for us. Or that the friends we've met in the program really care about our well-being and that their suggestions can be trusted.

T²
LISTENING

Wisdom will come to us when we are ready for it. When the student is ready, the teacher appears.

I will listen to my teachers today. No situation has to baffle me.

Give up! Give up trying to control others. Give up trying to figure out who is right and who is wrong in every situation. Give up trying to guess the outcome of even the tiniest circumstance. Give up trying to figure out what is right for us and everyone else.

Giving up doesn't mean life is over! On the contrary, it means we have decided to live our own lives only. However, until we turn over to God what is clearly God's domain, as Step Three suggests, we cannot know the peace that awaits us. It is not our assignment to plan others' lives. The purpose of our journey is not to try to control the lives or the experiences of those who are traveling alongside us, but to offer love and acceptance only; and in the midst of our experiences we'll sense God's plan for us.

To surrender is to discover real hope and then joy.

CONTROL

Surrendering to God, to the experience, to the moment, will give me the peace and joy I long for today.

It's unhealthy yet quite normal to feel stressed out. All of us are working, either in the home or out of it. We are maintaining relationships with many people, some of whom we are in frequent conflict with. We set goals that are unrealistic, or we procrastinate and feel ashamed. It is easy to close the day feeling like a failure, and that puts an edge on our attitude, an edge that too often inflicts unwanted pain on someone else.

Quieting our minds conserves our energy.

STRESS

People often tell us we're doing the best we can. But are we? Let's consider making one very small change that can profoundly influence how our lives unfold daily. The change? Getting quiet. In the midst of turmoil, we can get quiet. While trying to make a decision, we can get quiet. When someone is orally attacking us, we can get quiet. When we're close to attacking someone, we can get quiet. When we feel hopeless and unable to go forward, we can get quiet. Peace will come.

T^2 THINK BEFORE ACTING/TALKING

The program serves me in so many ways today. I am developing the habit of getting quiet before acting or speaking, and that is changing my life.

Step Seven suggests that we humbly ask God to help us with *our* shortcomings, not other people's. Perhaps we fail to see our shortcomings on many occasions, or, when we do see them, we self-righteously justify them. We have honed in on other people's shortcomings far more often. Nevertheless, we can discover our own if we begin tracking our inner feelings. They are excellent indicators of the behavior(s) we need to change.

Humility means being teachable.

With God's help we can change or give up any behavior that hinders our lives and relationships. We don't have to yell in anger or pout over hurt feelings. Withholding our love or plotting revenge can be removed from our bank of reactions. We can ask God for freedom from any behavior we no longer want. And if we are willing to be free of the behavior, it will be removed—on God's timetable.

If I really want God's help in getting free of troubling behaviors, I simply have to ask. Help will come.

Are we troubled because we often bear the brunt of someone's anger but say nothing? Do we frequently adjust what we think or say in order to get along better with someone else? If we are guilty of either, then we may be suffering from *codependency,* a condition for which there is a powerful antidote.

Codependency was a survival tactic.

It's not unusual to grow up worrying about and reacting to the feelings of others while stuffing our own feelings. Most of us have suffered guilt and shame as forms of discipline. We learned to align our feelings and opinions with those around us as a survival tactic. But we never felt good about it because it never felt honest. Even worse, our self-esteem languished.

The Fourth Step helps us define who we are. The more open and honest we become, the less willing we'll be to let others treat us unjustly. Knowing our values will empower us to share them. Sharing them will free us from codependency.

I don't have to be silent if mistreated. Today I will not harbor resentment; instead, I will express my feelings.

Good decisions require careful consideration.

We are continually making decisions. How we talk to and treat other people is a decision, as is being angry and resentful. How we treat ourselves is a decision. Asking for help and accepting it are decisions too. Working a Twelve Step program is perhaps one of the most important decisions we'll make in our lifetime. How much simpler all other decisions will seem when we use the program's principles as guides.

Decision making is not new. We've been doing it all our lives. But many of our decisions have not been beneficial to us or to the people we care about. For example, we may have chosen inaction. We may have chosen to take charge of someone else's responsibilities. We may have tried to make our decisions in isolation.

Now, however, we have help we can trust for making every decision. Sponsors, friends, our Higher Power—all are within easy reach. Taking even a moment to check out our plan with someone else will give us the information we need. The decision itself is up to us, but the insight of others is always available.

I will look for guidance for every decision I make today. I'll be careful not to make decisions for others.

Every day, we wonder what might be the best solution to a problem. Should we leave a relationship if the drinking doesn't stop? What will happen to an adult child in jail if we refuse to post bail? Can we stop phoning parents who continue hurting us? Even less dramatic problems are as troublesome in some respects because they keep us from living to our full potential right now, at this moment.

Fortunately, we have found a solution that will work for any problem. First we pray. Then we quietly wait, listening for the wisdom our Higher Power has promised us. Can it really be this easy?

Most of us had relied very little on prayer before joining this fellowship; thus at first we doubted prayer's power. Now our experiences and the example of other people have strengthened our belief. We willingly, even joyfully, turn to our Higher Power each day. And problems that used to baffle us lose their power. Our answers are revealed.

Prayer offers comfort; meditation offers answers.

T2
STEP
ELEVEN

I will turn to my God in prayer and meditation today. No problem, large or small, will trouble me for long.

An asset can become a defect.

T²
APPROVAL
SEEKING

A positive trait many of us share is that we are good managers—we handle our responsibilities at home and on the job efficiently. Often our self-worth is tied to the praise we receive from other people. But it's a short leap from being a good manager to handling responsibilities that clearly belong to someone else. When we make that leap, we suddenly turn an admirable asset into a defect.

Our propensity for taking over the responsibilities of others comes from our need to control and our desire for continued affirmation of our skills. Being good managers over some aspects of our lives wins us desired compliments. Thus we figure that managing other people's lives will guarantee us love!

But we learn in the Twelve Step program that the truth is quite different. Let Go and Let God, Live and Let Live, the Twelve Step program tells us. These slogans seem foreign at first. Watching others and learning from them, however, change how we see our purpose in life. The change feels good, in time.

Managing my own life is my only assignment today.

Do we need to be *restored to sanity?* The first time we read Step Two we probably rejected this idea. We no doubt knew people who were crazy but insisted we were not included among them. As our minds began to clear enough to hear the stories and the wisdom of the men and women who share our path now, we realized we had done many "insane" things over the years.

Results depend on our efforts.

We've always wanted other people to live by our rules, to fulfill our expectations. We think they should meet all our needs. And we're willing to be quietly manipulative or be loudly aggressive to get our way. Again and again, though, we fail to get what we want. Our efforts to control, however subtle, create resistance every time. The insanity is that we try again.

The program is teaching us that we don't have to try again, ever. We can simply stop an old behavior and accept others as they are. This profoundly changes the peace we feel in our interactions with others.

I can have either peaceful or stressful interactions with people I meet today. What develops depends on how I behave.

Taking an inventory reveals our progress.

We want to be perfect. When we're not, *which is always,* we are certain our friends and co-workers are sitting in judgment. We expect far too much of ourselves, and we expect no less from others.

We need the Twelve Step program. It can bring balance to our lives. The demands we have placed on ourselves have taken their toll: We seldom laugh. We worry far too often. We almost never have fun. We have made our lives hard work, and our attempts to control people and circumstances have made the lives of our loved ones hard work too.

The Big Book tells us that progress, not perfection, is expected. Why is that so hard to believe? Perhaps because we don't know what it means to make progress. But we are making it. Just coming to a meeting regularly is making progress. Every time we refrain from criticizing someone else's behavior we're making progress. Not taking ourselves quite so seriously even one time today is also progress.

My prayer today is to lighten up. I am as good as I know how to be at this stage of my growth. And that's progress!

Suffering from low self-esteem is common. Some of it may be blamed on growing up in families affected by alcohol or other drugs. Perhaps the criticisms heaped on us at school or in a bad marriage triggered it. We may have thousands of reasons for lacking a sense of our worth. The bottom line is, we were insecure and full of doubt—good breeding ground for the superstar achiever.

Overachieving may be symptomatic.

Much good occasionally comes from low self-esteem. Working really hard, excelling in many extracurricular activities, being available when a favor is asked—these are common characteristics of people with low self-esteem.

The program is spiritually based, and in it we are introduced to a Higher Power. Many of us didn't have one before, at least not one we relied on, to help us feel better about ourselves. We are learning to turn to our Higher Power every day for peaceful assurance that we are loved, that we are being taken care of. In time we'll grow to love ourselves, and then we'll be free of the need to overachieve.

I will accept my worthiness today and trust that my Higher Power has something wonderful in store for me.

Our Twelve Step program is the way to peace and sanity.

DETACHMENT

Most of us came into this program because we wanted to stop someone else from using alcohol and other drugs. We expected to learn how to do it. We wanted to talk about how awful our lives had been. We thought others would commiserate with us. How wrong we were! And how lucky.

Instead, we have gotten support for making changes in ourselves, not in someone else. We have learned that we can focus on the blessings in our lives. We know now that we can detach from *the other person's* behavior. We are learning to accept that each one of us has our own special journey. Moreover, we can experience a quietness within ourselves that we never knew was there. Peace and sanity have become our companions.

Today gives me another chance to leave others alone, count my own blessings, and revel in the joy of peacefulness. Peace and sanity are all mine if I want them.

Why is it so hard to do the very thing that would make life feel so much softer and more manageable? Most of our worries relate to what may happen in our future, and our regrets are over what has happened in our past. Between our worries and our regrets, we leave little time for our minds to rest and relish the flavors of the present.

Relish life, one moment at a time.

WISDOM

T² LIVING IN THE PRESENT

Reliving past traumas and projecting future ones tire us almost as much as the actual experiences. We gain nothing from our obsession to dwell on the past and the future. In fact, we lose a lot. We lose the message our Higher Power is trying to give us through the *present* experience when that experience does not capture our full attention.

In the present we get all our answers. In the present we find security and hope. In the present we get well.

I will bring my attention back to now *every time it wanders today. I'll feel my Higher Power's presence.*

With a little effort, assets can be enhanced.

When we prepare to work our first Fourth Step we shudder, certain we'll fail to discover a single asset. It's okay to ask other people how they did a Fourth Step and what assets they recognize in us. Getting over the resistance to doing this Step is what's important at this stage of our growth. We all have assets. Maybe they don't seem as numerous as our liabilities, but we can identify our assets and work to accentuate them each day.

It's easy to take other people's inventories, easier than taking our own. We had taken lots of inventories before discovering a Twelve Step program. But now we need to focus exclusively on our own inventory. We can't expect to change in ways that enhance our well-being if we don't give careful attention to all our parts. While it's true that some of our parts may be enviable already, other parts may need work. We can add them to the "enviable" list by practicing healthy ways of interacting every time we are tempted to be critical of others.

It becomes a challenge, one that we'll enjoy, when we decide to emphasize our assets, watching how they change our lives.

I will accentuate my positives today and have a lot more fun.

So many variables affect each person's behavior that it's not possible to fully understand others. Their perspective regarding any circumstance is influenced by all the other circumstances in their lives.

Time is wasted when we try to figure out another person's motives.

We need to accept people as they are, making choices about which relationships to cultivate and which to let go of. If others are unloving and disrespectful, why should we cultivate them as friends?

It's true, of course, that we can choose our friends, but we cannot choose our families. And many times our most difficult relationships are family ones. However, we can still apply the same principle. We can behave respectfully toward family members, but we don't have to look to them for the support our friends will happily give us. We don't have to let the behavior of family members decide what we think of them or us.

I will not second-guess anyone today. My own history is all I really know.

Being willing to ask our Higher Power for help is the first step to getting it. And God has no expectations of how we pray. There isn't a wrong way. Chatting with God as we would a friend is as appropriate as kneeling in church or beside our bed. We'll be changed by our efforts regardless of our process.

We can pray in whatever way we please.

PRAYER

We're developing many skills and new behaviors with the help of Al-Anon and other Twelve Step programs. Our lives are changing daily as a result. Some of our new program friends consider prayer the most important of all the tools we're getting acquainted with. It's certain that the more accustomed we are to relying on prayer, the more quickly we'll find calm in the midst of chaos.

Sponsors tell us to seek opportunities for prayer. If we need solutions to problems, prayer will help. If we feel anger or resentment against someone, praying for that person will help. If we want to feel better about ourselves, prayer will help. When prayer becomes habitual, we'll discover our lives have really changed.

I feel calm and guided when I begin my day in conversation with God. Remembering that this friend will never desert me comforts me.

Some of us are in the program because the drinkers in our lives are out of <u>control</u> and we feel crazy. Others of us come to the program certain that we are managing our lives very well but hoping to learn how to better manage someone else. For some of us, the addict may have stopped using, but the feelings of hopelessness remain. Whatever our reason for being here, we are in the right place.

Do we manage ourselves to the best of our ability?

The program can teach us a lot if we are willing to learn. The first test of our willingness is being able to accept our powerlessness over others. Surrendering to God the management of all the other people in our lives will free us to better manage ourselves. But what does that mean? It means taking no action that we haven't talked over with a friend *and* with God. It means always loving and never harming the people we care about. It means never giving up the belief that our journey has purpose.

I will pay more attention to my own behavior than someone else's today. Managing me will keep me plenty busy. If I do it well, I'll be happy.

*Being willing
to listen
wholly is a
quality worth
striving for.*

FRIENDSHIP

Our preoccupation with silent, ongoing dialogues about "what she said yesterday" or "what he may do later today" prevents us from *hearing* what a friend may be trying to tell us now. And it's our struggle to control the "hims and hers" in our lives that keeps us focused on the other person even when that person isn't present. The obsession to control gets in the way of our sanity and serenity. We miss living our *own* lives when we obsessively focus on how the significant people in our lives are living theirs.

We have heard at Twelve Step meetings that frequently our Higher Power's guidance comes to us through the loving words of friends. If we are not listening intently while in conversation with our friends, we will miss the message God has for us. That message is exactly what we need right now.

*I will focus on my friends today and listen.
Their words contain the thoughts that should
come to me.*

We really aren't so bad. But we haven't been faultless either. We are human. We make mistakes, we lie, we pretend we are different than we really are. And we don't like admitting our defects, because that forces us to acknowledge who we are, and we feel ashamed. We are certainly more adept at and comfortable with pointing out someone else's defects.

Taking full ownership of ourselves is a major step in recovery.

DEFSCTS of CHARACTER

It's profoundly important to learn that when *we see* another person's defect, we have just expressed one of our own as well. Accepting other people means not being their judge. That's hard for most of us. Recovery means changing whatever needs changing. That's why we are here. That's why we are reading these words.

I probably won't like all of me today. But taking on one defect at a time, I can change.

Loving thoughts make loving actions possible.

POSITIVE
THOUGHTS

Our thoughts hold our actions hostage. When we're angry, we lash out at other people, often innocent bystanders. If we're harboring self-pity, our sullenness punishes others. Resentments cling to us, tainting our relationships. In each case, our behavior reflects what's on our minds.

This isn't new information. We are what we think! But let's remember that thoughts are never forced on us. What we dwell on is by choice, however unhealthy it may be. We can dwell on love with as little fanfare as we can dwell on hurt or hate, but it will take concerted effort and lots of practice. Consider it a challenge that promises immense happiness. We can count on that absolutely.

Let's shake ourselves free of any thought that isn't enhancing our well-being or our relationships today and think of God and love instead. Discovering the power of our thoughts will change us forever.

My thoughts are not at the whim of anyone else. I think what I want to. My thoughts will be positive today.

Impulsively we get into conflicts because we don't stop and think first. If a friend is about to do something her way, rather than our way, we often want to interfere. How much simpler we'd make our lives if we'd ask ourselves, "How important is it anyway?"

How important is it?

No two of us share the same perception of any situation, and each of us is certain our perception is right. That leads us to meaningless conflicts. Most disagreements are irrelevant, at least in the "big picture." Why, then, must we participate in them? The good news is, we don't have to. "How important is it anyway?" gives us a moment's pause, and that's generally all we need to walk away.

Minding our own business would profoundly change our experiences. We'd soon discover that we had extra time to pursue personal goals if we gave up watchdogging everyone else.

Any conflict I get into is because I've forgotten to ask the simple question, "How important is it anyway?" I'll be mindful of this today and stop myself before I get into conflict.

Cultivating a sense of <u>humor</u> guarantees that we'll find more joy in living.

One of the first things we encountered at a Twelve Step meeting was laughter. That surprised many of us. We came to our first meeting angry, or sad, or desperate. We weren't in a laughing mood, that's for sure! We quietly thought, How can these people help? They surely don't have the kinds of problems I have. How wrong we were! And how fortunate that we kept coming to meetings and over time gained from their examples.

Laughter heals. We know that now. Before we found the Twelve Steps, however, we always took everything too seriously. We assumed that everyone else's behavior either reflected on us or was directed at us. How grandiose we were! How grandiose we can be again if we forget to apply the program's tools.

We aren't the center of the universe. Al-Anon and other Twelve Step programs have taught us that. But we do play a significant part in a Divine plan. We are getting the experiences that are right for us. Accepting them more lightheartedly, with an understanding that God is close by, allows us to see the humor in situations that may have disturbed us before. Having a good laugh changes us and our vision.

I will cultivate laughter today. Most situations are not that serious. My perception is what distorts them.

OCTOBER

We have had lots of practice, no doubt, defining other people's defects. Looking at their defects is far easier than looking at our own.

We avoid looking at ourselves out of shame and fear. Sometimes even arrogance. Asking others to share how they did a personal inventory will give us a pattern to follow. Beginning with our positive characteristics gets us over the hump of resistance, but we need to willingly look at our defects too. It's the defects that we want to change, but until we acknowledge them, we can't expect to change them.

One of the greatest blessings of this program is that we can learn how to change. Our defects are our stumbling blocks, and we can kick them out of the way.

Inventories define who we are.

DEFECTS of CHARACTER

I will watch for my defects today. Any I don't want, I don't have to keep! Accentuating my assets will help.

It is not easy to turn the other cheek. When someone treats us in a mean-spirited way, we want to retaliate, at least initially. But when we do, the effects are long-lived. Taking spiteful action, action that hasn't been carefully thought out, often creates more problems. We have come to the Twelve Step program for help. Let's accept it.

How other people treat us doesn't have to control us.

Getting help from the program means first being willing to *receive it.* That is often not as easy as it sounds. We have learned to cherish particular survival skills over the years; however, now that we are in the program, we are becoming willing to relinquish them. One survival skill we particularly cherished was "an eye for an eye," which never left the scales balanced. Let's discard it. We'll discover an exhilaration we didn't know we were capable of when we decide not to react, to turn the other cheek rather than let someone else's behavior control us.

REACTIONS

SELF-CONTROL

I can walk away rather than react to anyone else on my path today. No one has control over me unless I give that person control.

Those of us sharing this program are so fortunate. First, we have a set of suggestions for living with whatever comes our way. This means that no experience will be too much to handle and no person can intimidate us unless we let it happen. Second, we can look to our Higher Power for strength and comfort. We'll find both. Third, the Twelve Step principles will be internalized in time if we give them steady attention.

But to keep growing, we need to continue our commitment to meetings and newcomers. From them, we'll get concrete reminders of how we have changed. Our willingness to help newcomers begin their journey of growth will benefit us tenfold. Seeing hope in the eyes of others will remind us of our own blessings.

Each day we get the gift of hope.

SPONSORSHIP

Today I will offer to someone else a lesson I have learned from experience.

Accepting God's will takes courage.

Step Three is a stumbling block for many of us. We're afraid to turn our lives over to God for fear we'll be called to live in unimaginable ways like giving up a job or spouse.

Fortunately, the men and women who share their experiences with us at meetings relieve us of many worries. We learn from them what it means to turn over our lives. And we hear firsthand how much easier their days unfold when they let God decide what they should do. We learn to expect saner, quieter living, fewer anxieties, and far greater certainty of how to proceed in every situation.

Accepting God's will is all I need to do today. I won't feel alone. I will be safe every minute.

Many of us don't understand how to quiet our minds. We have grown accustomed to our minds racing from one thought to another and can't imagine any other existence. How would the people in our lives get along if we weren't constantly concerned and thinking about them?

We can appreciate a quiet mind.

SERENITY

Learning to let go of other people, as suggested by our program friends, will free our minds to be at rest. We will also discover that we have more energy for accomplishing our own life goals when we give up our obsessive thinking about other people's lives.

Being quiet gives us the opportunity to notice the beauty around us: the birds singing, the flowers blooming, the snow falling, the rain cleansing the air and the streets. And even more, the personal blessings we each have received. None of us has escaped God's reach.

Today I will notice how God has been present in my life. Being quiet will open a channel to that knowledge.

Every experience has something to teach us.

LESSONS

We're students every minute. And as a result, *we teach.* Even in the most difficult struggles, we're storing information that will help us or someone else at a future time. From our happy times as well as our tragedies we gain valuable, necessary insights.

We probably didn't know this when we first came into the program. And we may still forget it regularly. Fortunately, we are surrounded by people who help us remember that every experience has a purpose. Each journey is unique, and the lessons in every experience are by design and on schedule. God's plan for us has brought us here. God's plan for our future will take us wherever we need to be.

Our fears diminish when we know that God is in charge and that our journey is according to Divine design. Our assignment is simply to listen and learn and pass on to others what we've been taught.

What my experiences teach me today, God intends for me to learn. I'll look for the opportunity to share what I know with someone else.

How often have we repeated the same ineffective behaviors while expecting a different outcome? Most of us have become obsessed with thinking we can change another human being. We have gone to extreme lengths, yet despite our failures we haven't given up. That's insanity. Maybe we're not dangerous to innocent bystanders, but our actions don't enhance other people's happiness.

Insanity has many faces.

Fortunately, the program's founders had the wisdom to recognize that insanity has many gradations. They have helped us realize how out of control, how crazy, many of our actions have been. Nothing gives us relief like turning to a Higher Power does. Nearly as quickly as we turn our thoughts over to God, our obsession to control releases its grip on our lives.

It's not always easy to accept that our behavior is insane. Seldom are there blatant repercussions. Nonetheless, turning our lives and our loved ones' lives over to God will bring us peace. It will help us acknowledge the insanity of the past when we contrast that with the peace we feel today.

My behavior might not look insane today, but if I'm obsessed with what someone else is doing, I'm not acting sanely. My Higher Power can help me find peace.

We are so impulsive, so sure we are right. It causes us to speak before thinking, to act before reflecting, to argue before looking at a problem from someone else's perspective. Thus we are in conflict often, because we have not relied on a "moment away with God" before responding to a situation.

Our Higher Power can guide our actions.

GUIDANCE

T² THINK
BEFORE
ACTING/THINKING

However, we do have hope. We are learning how to live more quietly, more respectfully, more lovingly. And all because we are looking to our Higher Power for help in deciding how to react in every situation. Having to apologize repeatedly because we pushed our opinions on others can become merely a dim memory. How fortunate for us.

I will go slow today and let God guide my actions.

Most of us came into recovery because we wanted someone else to get sober. We expected to learn what we needed to do to make the other person change. What a surprise was in store for us! And what relief! We have learned that we can't make someone else change and that it's not our job. We are free of a heavy burden, which means we can focus on our own dreams for a change.

We can take charge of our own lives, not the lives of other people.

PERSONAL GROWTH

This may feel a bit scary at first. What are our dreams and goals? Maybe it has been years since we thought only of ourselves. The program will help us. The principles, the Steps, the members of the groups—all will act as wonderful guides. We will learn by other members' examples, and in time we will be examples for the newcomers.

Learning who we are, separate from the others in our lives, is the greatest gift of this program. It inspires us and makes us appreciate our uniqueness. We are coming to know we really matter.

I will learn more about myself today than I knew even yesterday. Every day will give me new awareness. The program will make the difference.

A question newcomers frequently ask is, "How long do I have to go to these meetings?" "Until you *want to*," the old-timers reply. At first we don't understand. But our lives begin to change because we are behaving in new ways, ways we've learned through the program.

Program meetings are like vitamins: our need for them is ongoing.

We've probably heard that *insanity* means doing the same harmful thing repeatedly but always expecting a different outcome. That's how we lived for years, no doubt. Now we have a new plan to live by and a new set of expectations. It's wonderful and so comforting to realize that our lives today and in the future can be far more rewarding and serene as the result of taking our "daily vitamin." Our growth and happiness will be ongoing if we make a commitment to the program.

My Twelve Step program gives me hope that today will be handled with ease. I will know what to do.

We have all been affected by a loved one's addiction. For some of us it meant being irresponsible, neglecting work, school, other family members, friends, ourselves. Being overly responsible was common too. Many of us got very good at doing for others what they should have done for themselves. Now we are learning to limit our reign of responsibility to only those tasks that clearly belong to us.

Being responsible only for ourselves is the assignment.

There are many explanations for why we became overly responsible, but worry was the big one. We wanted other people to think well of our families, and since each family member's behavior reflected on the entire family (or so we thought), we tried to cover each person's base of responsibility. What a job! It wore us out and was never finished.

Our lives are much simpler now, because the responsibilities we each need to handle can easily be completed today, with time to spare.

I will do only what's mine to do today. That way I'll help others grow too.

T²

Often we assume that the experiences we want are the most important ones for our development as human beings. But that may not be the case at all. Experiences that seem insignificant at the time, or ones that are not at all what we want, might prove to be key to our future growth. We are unfolding purposefully. Where today's experience takes us is quite by design.

No experience is without meaning.

T²
GOD'S PLAN

Most of us wish that at least some things could be different. Maybe we think we deserve a better job or a happier, sober marriage. Maybe our children rarely live up to our high expectations. We get trapped into thinking we deserve better. And perhaps we are getting a heavy share of tough experiences to handle. But God is always with us, and everything that comes to us is intended to contribute to the person we are becoming.

Our perspective can lead to appreciation or dread. Deciding to see every situation as a blessing would significantly change us and what happens in our lives.

I am living an adventure today. God will give me experiences that I need. I may want other experiences, but God's love guarantees I'll get what I need.

It's normal for us to desire the love and acceptance of the important people in our lives. We might have begun doing favors for friends as a way of securing their affection. We didn't realize that we were establishing a habit that served no one. It taught us that we were loved only if we had done something for that love. And it enabled other people to shirk responsibilities that were clearly their own.

Love doesn't mean always doing for other people.

The program is teaching us about love. We are *coming to believe* that we are loved just as we are by our Higher Power. A "performance" is never necessary. We are learning that merely listening to others in need is a lovable act. Sharing with them our own experience, as others have done for us, is an act of love. We are seeing that assuming responsibility for all the details of our own lives is empowering us, and it is instilling self-love too.

In the past very little of what we thought was love was really love. And for years our lives stayed much the same. Now the changes are frequent and sometimes profound. We're discovering more happiness than we ever thought possible.

I will make sure I'm not trying to buy love today through my actions. I know now what real love is.

OCTOBER 14

When we admit powerlessness, we gain power.

T² STEP ONE

At first the idea of being powerless scares us. We have fooled ourselves into thinking we have everything under control. Managing other people's lives, or trying to, has been a consuming passion. So of course, the First Step, admitting we are powerless, seems out of the question.

Getting honest with the facts of our lives enables us to see that we often failed when we tried to get others to do our bidding. Anger, self-pity, tears, and even threats succeeded only occasionally. Every time someone else had a different plan in mind, the chances he or she would follow ours were slim.

However, being powerless isn't the end of the world. In fact, it's a wonderful gift in disguise. Giving up our attempts to manage others gives us energy, lots of it, to use for our own benefit. And using all our power on ourselves means we can finish tasks we've put off, change a behavior that causes us grief, play more, or fulfill a dream we've kept in the back of our minds. We have more power over what we do.

I have all the power I want at my disposal today as long as I use it only on myself.

Many of us wandered into our first meeting afraid we'd see someone we knew who would find out that drug addiction had touched us. Being told that "whatever is said here, stays here" relieved us some, but we were still leery.

Anonymity makes it possible for anyone to receive help.

We discover early in our recovery that meetings are like a "safe house," a place where we can go and talk openly about who we are and the pain in our lives. Meetings are also a place where we can expect to receive the support we have craved for so long. Our backgrounds don't matter. What we do for a living is unimportant. We are people in need and in that way absolute equals.

Sharing the most intimate details of our lives with people whose last names we do not know awakens our sense of *sameness* with others. It's profoundly healing to acknowledge how alike we are.

I am on equal footing with everyone I meet in the program. Remembering that today will keep me humble and hopeful.

God's will and self-will are seldom compatible.

The Big Book tells us that alcoholism is "self-will run riot." But the alcoholic man or woman has no exclusive claim to this trait. We concerned others have extremely powerful wills too. We tried to control the chemically dependent person, our families, our co-workers, even strangers. We generally failed, but we didn't give up. We just pushed harder the next time.

When we feel strongly about something, how do we discern the difference between our will and God's? Our understanding about the difference comes slowly, but it does come, as long as we are willing to go within and acknowledge our feelings. If we are honest, we'll intuitively know what the will of God is. And if we are sincere about wanting the rewards of this program, we'll fulfill that will rather than our own.

I don't want my will to ruin my day. God has a wish for me in every circumstance today. I'll pay heed to God's will by listening closely to my inner voice.

The phrase "living in the present" isn't really mysterious or mystical, though it might sound that way at first. All it means is keeping our focus on whatever is happening right now, believing that's the specific experience God is giving us at this point in our lives. Twelve Step philosophy tells us we are always given what we need, when we need it. We can appreciate whatever is happening much more easily when we believe that.

Plan for the future, but live in the present.

LIVING IN THE MOMENT

But what about the future? We might need to change jobs or move to another home. Responsibly planning for future needs does not mean we have forsaken the present. There is a difference, and we do know when we are missing out on the moment by brooding over the past or fearing the future.

I will pay attention to my thinking today. If I'm caught in the past or the future, I'll bring myself back to the present.

We are hopeful, not hopeless.

·HOPE

It's not unusual to be filled with despair by the time we seek help. It seemed necessary to try, on our own, to change the alcoholic. Managing that person's responsibilities, emotions, and relationships had become our lives. We had an intense desire to transform the alcoholic into our image of what he or she should be. Repeatedly failing to do so forced us finally to give up the effort. The resulting despair was overwhelming. It was also a habit.

It seems a miracle that the despair has gone. What's changed? All we do differently is come to meetings, talk to sponsors and trusted friends, and stay out of other people's business. Yet everything is changed. The tension is gone from our lives and relationships; we feel hopeful rather than hopeless; and we are certain that we will be okay, regardless of what others around us are doing. Maybe a miracle is at work. Or maybe just letting others be in charge of themselves is the catalyst for change. All that matters is that despair is gone for as long as we focus on ourselves.

I am despairing only when I'm too lazy to take charge of my mind. I'll remember that today.

Everybody loves giving advice, but no one really loves getting it. Advice often sounds like control, and we want to be free to make our own decisions. However, we can appreciate hearing what worked for other people, and we aren't intimidated by shared experiences. It behooves us to remember this when we are about to give advice to newcomers.

Sharing what worked for us is far better than giving advice.

Remembering how it was for us when we first came to meetings will help us know how to approach others who are hurting as we were hurting when we first sought help. Confusion, hopelessness, and fear haunt every newcomer. The way others enfolded us in their hope when we had none made it possible to survive one day at a time. It's our turn now to pass on that hope to others.

The real gift in telling about our experiences rather than giving advice is that we too are strengthened each time we remember how far we have come.

I will be available to help a friend today. My experiences are all I really know, but that's quite enough.

We can let go of someone else's behavior.

LETTING GO

RELIEF

How many times did we anguish when a loved one disappeared from sight during a party? How many times did we try to keep someone from taking one more pill or mixing one more drink? Sometimes we even succeeded in stopping someone from using alcohol or other drugs. But the win was short-lived. Finally we had to let go.

Despite our initial reluctance at giving up the burden of trying to control others, we now know it feels good. Coming to believe that we each have a Higher Power has helped. We can let that Power do the work we were trying to accomplish but couldn't. This frees us to fill the hours of our days with activities that deserve our attention.

I will back off from trying to control anyone but myself today. The only behavior that is a reflection on me is my own.

Presumably, we came to the program because we wanted help. Our hopelessness had stolen our enthusiasm for work and play; our vision of the future was bleak. Our first meeting gave us some relief: At least we could see that other people had lived through similar experiences.

Justifying our behavior allows us to stay stuck.

We didn't change our behavior overnight, though. We still complain about the alcoholic, whether he or she is drunk or sober. Our actions are often automatic—requiring no decision making. And we hang on to these actions even after hearing our sponsors and others say it's time to change.

It's not easy to give up familiar behaviors, even ones that usually backfired on us. But the experiences of the others in our meetings are the encouragement we need. Although justifying the old behavior may be easier than working on new behavior, it won't change our hopelessness to hopefulness. That's why we're here.

I can't expect my life to get better if I keep responding in the same ways to whatever happens. I am learning the tools for changing me. I'll use them today!

Twelve Step principles simplify life.

Creating crises came easily for most of us. We worried about bills, the family, the neighbors, our jobs, who was drinking and how much. It seemed to be our job to control the opinions and the behavior of everyone who crossed our path, and we got angry when other people wouldn't give in to our demands. Painful turmoil dogged our steps. Unhappiness seemed our destiny.

Recovery has changed all that. At first we wonder how such a simple program made up of ordinary people can cause such profound change. The answer lies in the spiritual aspect of the Steps. Coming to believe in a Higher Power and then letting that Higher Power take charge of our will and our lives means we are willing to give up our control of others. It also means we can be at peace rather than in crisis. No longer are we in charge of anyone or anything else. And that's what simplifies life.

My life will be both simple and peaceful today if I let God take charge of others.

Excusing chemically dependent people's behavior, particularly by covering up for them, doesn't help them recover. Neither does shaming. It's an illness we're dealing with, one that has them in tow, and only their willingness to recover coupled with God's grace can make that possible. However, there are certain actions we can take.

Addiction is an illness, not an act of revenge.

SELF-FOCUS

We can pray for their recovery, just as we pray for the well-being of our other loved ones. We can focus on the positive details in their lives. We can work our own program of recovery, utilizing the help of our Higher Power. We can practice expressing love even during those times when we'd rather be mad or judgmental. We can assess our own behavior honestly, making amends where they are called for. We can single out one of our assets and strengthen it by using it more often.

Putting the focus on ourselves and the ways we need to change rather than on the alcoholic will let others come to terms with their own illness, a first step for their recovery.

I will look at myself today. Judging the alcoholic or addict, or anyone else, does not contribute to my well-being.

What if we knew what lay ahead?

FAITH

Anxiety can immobilize us: Will she get home safely? Did he lose his job this time? Do they want me to move out? Does he really love me? The consternation is unending for some of us. We keep our minds agitated worrying about the unknowns. Eventual freedom from anxiety is one of the gifts of coming to the program for help.

Had someone told us a few years ago that we'd end up here, we wouldn't have believed them. If someone told us now what was in store for us ten years into the future, we would probably not believe them either. God gets us ready for our experiences a little at a time. With practice, we can learn to trust that we'll be able to handle whatever lies ahead. We'll know that God is never separate from us. All experiences are designed for our growth and are part of God's plan. We're not in charge, but we are being taken care of.

If I begin to worry today, I'll know that I have forgotten that God is and will always be my protector. All is well.

Sometimes we were smug and passed judgment on other people, certain that we'd never be in their circumstances. However, most of us never thought we'd be in our current circumstances either. We simply can't know what the future holds for us, and if we did we'd probably be terrified, certain we couldn't handle whatever burdens we might have to bear.

But for the grace of God . . .

WORRY

It's no accident that we're in a Twelve Step program. We couldn't have imagined this as a necessary part of our lives a few years ago, but it is, and our lives have begun to feel purposeful and guided. Developing trust that a Higher Power has always been in charge gives us confidence that we'll not be led into waters so troubling that we can't wade through them.

Our lives feel so much freer now. Remembering that God's grace has brought us to this point can relieve us of the compulsion to worry about the future.

My Higher Power has saved me thus far. I am confident that I will be protected today too.

*I am
responsible
for myself
only.*

CARETAKING

Often we have taken care of other people's responsibilities quite innocently. We saw jobs that needed to be done so we did them. On many occasions, however, we took charge of a task as a way to manipulate someone or to make ourselves look good. Too much of our self-worth came from doing, doing, doing. The boundary between our own work and someone else's was blurred.

Recovery, by contrast, involves learning to be responsible for the minute details of our own lives. At first glance this appears more difficult for the alcoholic or addict than for us. But we must focus on ourselves only.

Letting others do for themselves takes vigilance. We must recognize our tendency to cross the boundary into someone else's territory. And we must remember to honor boundaries.

F²

*I will ask my Higher Power to help me do only
what needs to be done by me today. It may not
be easy, but my willingness will help.*

It's not unusual at a meeting to hear someone say, "I believe in God. I just don't trust God to do my will." Much of the trouble in our lives may have happened because we attempted to force outcomes that were not in God's plan for ourselves or our loved ones.

Believing and trusting in a Higher Power are not the same thing.

TRUSTING GOD

The program will help us. The Steps are laid out quite specifically. First we accept our powerlessness. Then we become willing to believe in a God of our choosing. And then we turn our wills and lives over to God. That requires trust. Initially, we may have to simply pretend we trust. But enough practicing will convince us that God's care, as the Step suggests, is always in our best interest. Hindsight will convince us, if we're willing to see it.

The real gift of believing and trusting in a Higher Power is that the hard work is done for us. We get to observe our lives falling into place. We become less hassled and more serene.

I can trust God only if I'm willing. Today, if necessary, I'll act as if I trust God. The payoff will come over time.

It's common to be angry by the time we discover Al-Anon or other Twelve Step programs for family members. We tried everything imaginable to get other people to stop their destructive behavior. We failed but all along felt certain we were right.

Anger doesn't win battles.

Now we're learning that we can't possibly know what's right for someone else. Other people's paths are being defined by them and their Higher Power; our path is being defined by us and our Higher Power. The program is helping us to make this distinction and focus solely on our path.

We don't shed our anger overnight, but the stories others tell at meetings give us new perspective and ultimately a willingness to consider giving it up. We are coming to understand how unproductive anger is. It has kept us from pursuing far more worthy goals.

If I begin to feel angry today, I'll remember that it helps no one and actually harms me. I'll give it up.

It's quite common for newcomers to assume that attending Al-Anon or another Twelve Step program won't be necessary once the alcoholic gets sober or the addict gets clean. Discovering, as we all do, that many members have been coming to meetings for years is startling. What's the point? we wonder. We expect the details of our lives to run smoothly as soon as sobriety takes hold.

The addict is clean. Why am I still unhappy?

HAPPINESS

The reality doesn't match our expectations. We still get into battles with people, have bouts of depression, worry about what could happen: all this despite the addict's being clean and sober! Little by little, it sinks in that our problems are ours; they are not caused by the alcoholic or anyone else. And the solutions lie within us. Whatever someone else does, we are still responsible for our feelings.

Once we get used to the idea of being fully responsible for how we feel, it exhilarates us. We can be happy if we want to be, regardless. No one can steal it from us. That's real power—and it's ours.

I can benefit from the program forever. As long as I use the tools I've learned, I'll never need to worry that I'll forget how to be happy.

Perfection as a goal is a setup for failure.

What does it mean to be "perfect"? Would we recognize it? We're exposed to the near-perfect performances of star athletes and entertainers nearly every day. Yet they miss shots on the court, putts on the green, and high notes on the trumpet, despite working hard to perfect their chosen skills.

Being human precludes the possibility of being perfect. But how often do we get mad or ashamed of ourselves for making a mistake? Errors unforgiven multiply. That's because the shame we harbor over our imperfections affects our attitude. The more we think we should be perfect, the greater our chances of failure.

We have come to the right place for help. Meetings are filled with people who share our struggle to be perfect. We'll grow to love the easy laughter over the failings we all have. And we'll learn that the more we can accept our human failings, the less often we'll have them.

Doing my best and accepting it as good enough are as close to perfection as I need to come today.

There are times when we feel overwhelmed by our shortcomings. And it seems that most of our friends have few, if any. Of course, that too is one of our shortcomings: We compare ourselves with other people and never quite measure up.

Changing one thing at a time is quite enough.

CHANGE

We each are a collection of assets and shortcomings. That's the human condition. But we can strengthen the traits we like and de-emphasize the rest. We just can't do it all at once.

First, we choose one element of our behavior, either an asset or a defect. Then we decide what we want to do with it today. There is a perfect formula for making changes in our lives. Keeping our focus small and our expectations reasonable allow us to experience the success we deserve. Little by little, applying this formula regularly, we will become the people we envision ourselves to be.

I am much more than whatever shortcoming caused me pain yesterday. Today is a new day, and I can help one of my assets blossom by demonstrating it repeatedly.

NOVEMBER

Hoarding possessions, money, or even information becomes a way of life for many people. "He who dies with the most wins" is a saying we may have laughed over. We see how silly our need for more is, but we often still fall prey to hoarding, in whatever form it presents itself.

The more love we give, the more love we receive.

A principle of the Twelve Step program is to give away what we have gained. This doesn't mean money or possessions. Giving things away is a mind-set many of us need to cultivate. And that's exactly what this program asks us to do.

We are learning from the old-timers that offering other people love, understanding, a willingness to listen, acceptance, hope, and patience means we'll get back the same and more. The less we hoard, the more we have. That's a promise we can count on.

I will look not to get but to give today. My reward is guaranteed.

This fellowship's support makes every experience easier to handle.

We had to do everything alone. Or so we thought. Our problems caused us lots of anxiety, but we feared asking other people for help. We didn't want them to know our situation or our inadequacies. Keeping our problems to ourselves kept others from knowing who we really were. We thought, surely if they really knew us, they wouldn't like us. That's how we lived for years. What a relief not to have to live that way anymore.

Keeping no secrets makes life so much simpler. We don't have to guard our words, being careful of what we tell to whom. Letting others know who we really are gives us the opportunity to experience genuine acceptance. And we are learning every day that these new friends love us just as we are. More importantly, we are learning that we are not all that different from them. This wonderful fellowship is changing all of our lives.

FELLOWSHIP SUPPORT

Sharing my struggle, whatever it may be, with a friend today diminishes its control over my life.

The more we trust our Higher Power, the less we need to put ourselves above other people. We are growing in our understanding that each of us has a significant part to play in the lives of everyone we touch. We are equal in value. In God's view no one is superior—or inferior.

Acting superior may have become a habit. The momentary lift we get from putting someone down draws us back to old behaviors. However, it's like an addiction to alcohol, sex, or food. We're only satisfied ever so briefly, and then we seek the superior feeling again.

Getting free of the need to feel superior is one of the blessings of this program. Drawing closer to our Higher Power is the tool we can use to accomplish this goal.

Acting superior is a sign of our low self-esteem and our distance from God.

SUPERIORITY

The people I see today have something of value to teach me. I am their student and God is in charge.

The absence of love is fear.

Fear haunts many of us. Fear of what the alcoholic in our lives is doing, fear of what the neighbors think, fear of losing our job, fear of being abandoned—the list is endless. It's the lack of connection to a Higher Power that invites the fear in. Yet when we feel God's presence, we can bask in the warmth of love, giving it and receiving it. And fear is gone.

Admittedly, we don't always feel God's presence, even when we ask "for knowledge of God's will." But a tool this program has given us—acting as if—can help. When we act as if we feel love for our companions and co-workers, we begin to feel at peace, connected to God, and the fear dissipates. The wonderful realization is that we don't have to feel God's presence first to be loving; we can get to God through having faith that His love will replace our fears.

I will shed any fears I have today by making the effort to love the people around me. My Higher Power will be close too.

To listen should be easy. It requires us to take no action, to make no monumental decision. It simply means getting quiet, freeing our minds of the clutter that carries us from one imagined scenario to another, and focusing on the sacred words of the speaker.

Listening is the best gift we can give another person.

We are all truly sacred beings, divinely placed here at this time. That's a fact. There isn't any more important activity at this moment in time than to be attentive to the person God has placed in our path. Listening with all our hearts will open us to God's special messages.

When I listen I honor and respect the special "inhabitants" of my life.

Believing in God is not the same as actually relying on God to help us travel through life. As children, many of us recited, "Now I lay me down to sleep. . . ." But few of us remembered throughout the day that God was present. We grew to adulthood afraid and confused about many experiences because we did not know how to "turn over" our troubles to God.

We can learn to rely on a Higher Power.

T.² GOD TRUSTING

What a different perspective we can have now on most experiences if we see them through the eyes of our Higher Power. In years past, we didn't realize what we were missing. Most things scared us. Before taking God as our companion, as our program suggests, we struggled with even the small stuff. Now the big stuff is manageable too.

I feel at peace. I am free from confusion. No fear is too big when I let my Higher Power help. Today will be good.

Each of us who comes to a Twelve Step meeting harbors at least a tiny fear, initially, about the safety of sharing secrets that have kept us stuck. Some of us have haunting memories of earlier times when our disclosures weren't kept in confidence. Today, however, as we listen to the openness and honesty of other people, we are assured that this is a safe place—to be and to share.

"What we hear here, stays here."

CONFIDENTIALITY

Having a place we can go to unburden ourselves begins the healing process, perhaps even before we have begun to share. Just knowing we can talk freely as soon as we are ready, that we have friends who want to listen and help, diminishes the seduction of isolation. And that's where we have lived for a long time.

Keeping the secrets divulged by friends in a meeting creates a bond, one that is strengthened with each disclosure. For many of us, this is the first time in our lives we have felt needed, listened to, and equal to the people around us. What a blessing this program is!

I will keep all my conversations confidential today. I want others to trust me just as I want to trust them.

There is a Divine plan for our lives.

While in the midst of turmoil, we sometimes forget that our Higher Power is available to ease the pain. We need to remember that whatever we experience is for our growth and is part of God's plan that is unfolding in our lives, a plan that feels painful simply because we forget that God is the architect.

Taking time every day to reflect on the past and the changes we've survived will help us acknowledge that a plan has been unfolding. Most of us are in a safer, better spot now than ever before. The myriad worries have been resolved. We have the support of genuine, loving friends. No experience, no matter how trying, has to be handled alone. And this is all part of God's plan.

I will eagerly remember that God is orchestrating my life today. Every experience is part of the Divine plan.

It's not easy to give up our obsession to control other people. We have lived with it for many years. It has even served us well, we think. So why have we ended up here?

Twelve Step meetings were never on our list of hoped-for destinations. And initially we doubted that we needed them. Some of us went to satisfy a counselor, others because a trusted friend suggested going. Whether it was our children, spouses, or friends who were in trouble with alcohol or other drugs, help, we were told, was available from the program.

But what kind of help do we need? We're not sure at first. We are still functioning. We seldom miss work, meals get prepared, and clothes get washed. The fact that we're angry or feeling sorry for ourselves isn't such a big deal. "Who wouldn't, if they lived with our families!" we say. If only "they" would do what we want them to do, we certainly wouldn't need the program.

The journey that others must make is neither for our review nor for our approval. Wishing them well, period, is all that's asked of us. The program can teach us how to do that.

How did we end up here?

CONTROL

Are my wishes for a friend sincere today? Or am I trying to protect myself in a subtle, dishonest way? If I stick close to the Twelve Step principles, I'll know the difference.

Compassion is not pity.

Being pitied makes us feel not only insignificant and powerless but also subtly shamed. While it's natural to want understanding and emotional support from other people, we need to see how clearly different these feelings are from pity.

Since we are in a program where we share experience, strength, and hope, we can learn from each other the difference between pity and compassion. We'll begin to realize that when others have compassion for us, it quietly empowers us to keep moving ahead, to stay hopeful. On the other hand, pity seems to escalate our hopeless feelings. What's more, our pity and anger certainly never inspire change in chemically dependent loved ones. Our compassion, however, may be the impetus they need to have hope in themselves.

I will look for opportunities to express compassion today. They will be my chances to inspire hope, which may be followed by change.

Giving up seemed like failure before we learned the principles of this program. We were probably taught that perseverance pays. In some cases it does. For instance, we profit from persevering in school or on the job. However, when we use perseverance to try and control anyone else's thoughts or actions, we are headed for *real* failure coupled with real pain.

Surrendering to a Power greater than ourselves is life-enhancing.

SURRENDER

Since most situations in our lives involve other individuals, we are experiencing the uncontrollable most of the time. That is when we can benefit most from turning the situation over to our Higher Power. We will feel great joy when we learn how easy it is to "give up."

I will practice "giving up" today every time I am drawn into a power struggle.

Start with an asset.

Secrets make us sick. We get paranoid, certain that other people must suspect "the truth" about us. We isolate out of fear, and our secrets loom even larger. But the Steps offer a solution. Step Four, for example, suggests we honestly outline who we are and how we behave, listing both our good and bad traits. Step Five asks us to tell what we learn about ourselves to another person and to God.

These Steps are big ones, so it's best if we take them a little at a time. Start with an asset. We all have assets. Maybe it's our sense of humor. Writing our assets down on paper gets us over the hump of resistance, and fear begins to leave us. Little by little, we let who we are emerge on paper. And we discover we're not so bad after all.

Telling God and someone else all our secrets may seem harder. Let's trust our friends rogram who say we will benefit im- bly. A terrible weight will be lifted r shoulders, and we'll no longer feel from the human family. Healing can ith self-disclosure.

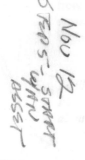

what I can for my own healing today. egin by being honest with other people ho I really am.

Worrying about the future—whether our focus is on this afternoon or next summer—is behavior we're free of if we work the program. One of the first slogans we are introduced to is One Day at a Time. Remember how baffling that idea was at first? We wondered how we could possibly not worry about what *might* happen. Now we know it's possible.

Live One Day at a Time.

How did we get from our incessant worrying to nearly full-time freedom from worry? Most of us came to believe that a Higher Power was taking care of us and all the matters we worried about. It takes vigilance, however. We can easily fall back into the old habits if we don't utilize the principles we've been taught. Today is all there is right now. We are in good hands right now. Tomorrow will take care of itself when it becomes right now.

Today is it. God is with me. All is well.

Looking for good in other people improves our attitude.

JUDGMENT

We weren't born critical and negative. We developed those behaviors. And for many of us they became habit. They also became self-defeating. If we saw only the faults and not the assets in others, we probably assumed they saw the same in us. We were all losers in the process.

We have come to the program because we are tired of losing! We want to feel better about ourselves; one of the easiest ways to accomplish this is to feel better about others. It's really not so difficult to see the better side of others. Initially it's a decision. Then it's willingness to practice the behavior. The hardest part is bringing our minds back to the positive when they wander through their old stomping grounds.

Asking God for help will begin the process of change for us. Not dismissing even the smallest positive quality in another will improve our perspective.

I will see only the good in my friends today. Practice will help.

Every day we will experience a situation that we wish were different. Sometimes it will be serious, such as the loss of a job or a dear friend or the relapse of a spouse. But even minor turbulence can cause us a setback emotionally. An angry clerk, a reckless driver, a crying child—all can move us from our peaceful center if we let them.

Choose to learn from life's pitfalls.

The program is teaching us another way to respond to pitfalls—the Serenity Prayer— which tells us to accept what we cannot change and change what we can. And we can always change how *we* perceive a situation. We can learn from and live with even the most dire circumstances if we cultivate an attitude of acceptance. It may sound difficult at first, and we may resist simply because we are accustomed to thinking things should go our way. But we can be peaceful in the midst of any disturbance if we make that choice.

I will be careful about the choices I make today. My happiness depends on it.

November 16

Thoughtful action is different from the more common reaction.

It became our habit to react to grave or even ordinary situations before considering what the best, most loving response might be. We jumped to conclusions. This left us far more troubled than if we had exerted some restraint. Simply taking a five-second pause and quieting our minds will positively influence the outcomes of most circumstances of our lives.

We do want peaceful, happy lives or we wouldn't have come to Twelve Step recovery. We seek the serenity we observe in others. We crave the joyful attitude and the heart full of hope that our friends here have. We know they haven't learned anything that is beyond our mastery. Imitating their approach to life's currents will immediately introduce us to a more peaceful life.

PEACE

RESTRAINT

T² REACTING RATHER THAN ACTING

T² THINK BEFORE ACTING/TALKING

I will slow down today. Pausing for a few seconds before saying or doing anything will have immediate payoffs.

The first time someone tells us to "let go" we're baffled. We come into this program hanging on so tight to others that we're no longer aware of it. Our attempts to <u>control</u> people and outcomes have become our way of life.

Letting go is an ongoing commitment.

Through the Second Step we begin developing trust in a Higher Power. Then we begin to sense what letting go means. We are coming to believe a Higher Power will take care of all those situations that worry us and all those people we've tried to manage.

T² Step Two

It's very common to think we have let go only to discover we still have a tight grip. Perseverance is called for. This is a major change for us, and we'll have to be vigilant in our efforts to let others do as they will and let God do what's called for in others' lives. Let's not give up hope when we find we've taken back that which we thought we'd given up. We're normal, and this is a program of progress, not perfection.

I will focus on only my life today. Trying to control what anyone else is doing will frustrate both of us.

Joy is evident in many faces at Twelve Step meetings.

We wonder how people who still live with loved ones' alcoholism and addiction can possibly feel joy. That's not how we feel, at least when we first come to this program. It's hard to be happy when others aren't doing what we want them to do! We discover after only a few meetings that we have a lot to learn. We also discover that the program is filled with excellent teachers.

Giving up trying to control other people, as Step One suggests, is the first lesson we're introduced to. What relief that provides! We get our first glimmer of joy as soon as we dare to experience "giving up." Letting God into our lives, as the Second and Third Steps suggest, gives us more opportunities for joy. And then the floodgates open! The program teaches us that we can feel joy if we're willing to change, even a bit at a time, how we see and accept others, how we take charge of ourselves, how we share what we have learned.

Joy is not exclusively held by a few. Each of us can find it, feel it, savor it, maintain it, and give it away. The Twelve Step approach is the key.

If I'm not feeling joyful today, I am not utilizing the lessons I've been taught in the program. I can turn my day around now if I want to.

Worry becomes a habit. Many of us began developing this habit when we were children. "Will we be loved?" "Will we pass the test?" When we grew up we continued to worry about all kinds of things—someone else's behavior, the traffic, the weather, our relationships, our abilities. The content of our worries was not particularly relevant, but the nature of our behavior was.

The future is in God's hands.

Before our introduction to Twelve Step recovery we seemed to think that we could control what happened if we worried enough about it. Our thinking is clearer now, and we can see that our worrying never guaranteed anything. It just kept us agitated.

Coming to believe that the future as well as the present is in God's hands relieves us of the *need* to worry. However, giving up worry is not easy. It has become second nature to us, yet with dedicated practice we can give it up.

I will give my worries to God today. I want my mind free so I can be creative and joyful. I want to laugh and feel grateful.

Feeling hopeful is a choice.

Wringing our hands over another person's behavior never helps the situation. Neither does nagging, at least not for long. Our interference, in even the most subtle ways, won't guarantee the outcome we're certain is best. At times it feels as if we have no recourse. But we always have one: prayer.

It may seem lame to rely only on prayer when our friends and loved ones are struggling with the demons of addiction. Yet it's helpful to remember that we can never control the actions someone else is taking or control the journey someone else is making. Remember, other people have a Higher Power watching over them, just as ours watches over us. Prayer coupled with hope is the most fruitful action we can take on behalf of our loved ones. God and destiny will do the rest.

I will stay hopeful today on behalf of my friends and other loved ones. I will turn them over to the care of their own Higher Power.

How quick we are to blame someone else for our anger or our hurt feelings. Blaming other people is easy. What's hard is accepting that our thoughts cause our feelings. Our program friends will help us see that taking responsibility for our thoughts and feelings empowers us to change our lives in dramatic ways. And none of us came into this program content with our life.

Feelings are triggered by thoughts.

It may seem grandiose to think we can change our lives. But we can. We can change the content of our minds, which in turn changes the feelings we harbor. We choose how we see a situation. We choose how we react to a set of circumstances. We are in charge. Being happy is a choice.

I can't blame anyone else for how I feel today. My thoughts are in charge of that.

Al-Anon and other Twelve Step programs help us live one day at a time.

Living one day at a time makes every situation tolerable. We came to this <u>program</u> for help because of a chemically dependent person's drinking and other drug use. We stay because the principles help us handle every aspect of our lives.

In fact, alcohol or other drug use is no longer present in many of our homes, and sometimes friends ask, "Do you still need the program?" What a good opportunity for us to recall what it was like, and what it's like now. Without the program, we'd still be trying to control the uncontrollable. We'd still be "doing" everyone else's life as well as our own. We'd still be lying to ourselves, to neighbors, to other family members, and to bosses about the condition of the alcoholic in our lives. We'd still be missing out on the gifts inherent in letting go and letting God. The program is a way of life. Miraculously, it has given us our lives back.

Remembering what it was like then and being grateful for what it is like now are a good exercises for me today.

No matter what other people do or say, they can't make us act against our will. We'd love to blame them for our outbursts or sadness. We're certain that if they would behave differently, we'd be different too. While it might be true that how someone behaves affects us, it doesn't have the power to take over our lives. How we react is still wholly up to us.

Situations don't have to trigger regrettable reactions.

A key element of recovery is learning the breadth of our personal power. We are in charge of who we will be and what we will do every minute of our lives. The statement "He made me do it" is simply never true. Taking full responsibility for our reactions requires honesty and willingness, both of which come more easily when we get accustomed to working the Twelve Steps. Initially, it may seem easier to blame others than to take full charge of ourselves. But we'll grow to love the empowerment that accompanies being responsible for all our actions, and we'll never want to trade that for our old lives.

I won't blame anyone for how I feel today. And how I behave will be my decision too. Being fully in charge of myself makes me feel strong and competent. I am excited about today.

Good decisions depend on good ideas from other people.

→ IMPULSIVITY

When a crisis occurred, we often acted on impulse. Occasionally our impulses were sound. However, they often complicated the crisis, and we were left with fear or frustrations.

It shouldn't surprise us that we handle situations that way. For most of our lives we relied solely on ourselves. When a problem arose, we took care of it or denied it. Looking to other people for help or even suggestions meant we were inadequate. We had invested far too much in trying to make ourselves look good; thus we couldn't let a problem derail our image.

Twelve Step programs can help us develop new patterns for handling problems. Solutions often emerge from our conversations with others. Sometimes the answers become clear during prayer and meditation. We are finally getting free of our anxiety about what others think. We know our program friends aren't judging us; they have a sincere interest in passing on the help the program has already given them. Their ideas, mixed with our willingness to listen and trust, guarantee us good decisions from now on.

My decisions today will be as good as the ideas I seek—from God, from friends, from the solace within.

Isolating ourselves was how we used to handle the pain and worry that plagued us. We paced the floor, cried, maybe drank too much, yelled at friends or children. But we seldom looked to other people for help. And even more seldom did we pray for the knowledge of God's will in our affairs. Being alone with our troubles was all we knew.

We are never alone.

Support

What a difference Twelve Step wisdom has made. Now we know we are never alone. We have learned, in fact, that we *were* never alone—we just didn't know how to let our Higher Power help before. We have also learned how to let friends share our burdens. No situation is quite so devastating when two are shouldering the pain.

I will reach out to someone today if I begin to worry. I'll remember to ask for God's help too.

Gratitude releases us from a negative attitude.

Once we break through our resistance to feeling happy, we discover a flood of joy for the *grace* that is ours. We are coming to know that we are here, now, by design. We understand that our lives have prepared us for the journey ahead.

Deciding to be grateful for our situation, our experiences, our unique perspective, quickly changes our outlook on everything that did happen, on everything that is happening now, and on everyone we meet. Accepting that we are in charge of whatever kind of day we will have forces us to accept responsibility for our joy, which can always be ours, or our unhappiness. And being grateful feels so good.

Gratitude is an attitude. I can feel it whenever I want. I will make a short list today of things I am grateful for.

Needing to be right drives us to argue. Why must we always be right? Our self-esteem is at stake. When other people don't share our views, we interpret that as meaning we aren't smart or clever enough. We take it as a personal affront, rather than simply a difference of opinion.

Arguments are losing propositions.

ARGUING

Program literature and meetings are helping us recognize that we each perceive life a bit differently. As we grow accustomed to listening nonjudgmentally to others share their experiences and perceptions, we begin to see beyond our own narrow opinions.

Letting others have their viewpoint frees us from the worry and tension of trying to be in control. In time we'll even feel enriched by the variety of opinions that surround us. When we accept those opinions as appropriate for the person who holds them, we will be changed immeasurably.

I can refrain from arguments today. Another's opinion doesn't define anything about me. Only my actions do that.

We have been given a second chance.

TO FORGIVENESS

Being human means making mistakes. No doubt we could have been better parents, better lovers, better employees, surely better children. But we were good enough! Forgiving ourselves for our past transgressions will free us to find more serenity in our present lives. We don't have to let our mistakes, or anyone else's, hold us back any longer. The program gives us new ideas about how to live, and it gives us new principles to live by. It gives us another chance for finding well-deserved joy.

Staying stuck in the past is always a choice. We see people at meetings who seem to have made that choice. Fortunately, we also see the winners. They are the ones who have grateful attitudes. They spread joy just by their presence. They refuse to say "I can't." They offer hope and help if we want it. Watching them, listening to them, and following their example guarantee we'll find our second chance, just as they have.

I am here because I want another chance at happiness. All I really have to do is take it.

We come into the program certain that we'd be happy if only the alcoholic would quit drinking. Surprisingly, he or she often does, and then we discover we're still unhappy. Our problem isn't the alcoholic. While it might be true that living with an alcoholic can be stressful and his or her behavior can complicate our plans, *we* decided to give up our happiness. The alcoholic never took it from us.

The alcoholic isn't the problem.

T2

ATTITUDE

Meeting with other people who are content, even joyful, in spite of sharing their lives with an active alcoholic gives us valuable food for thought. Happiness is a by-product of how we live our lives, not how others live theirs. Giving the drinker or the boss or the noisy neighbor power over how we feel is always an option, but the payoff is not what we really want.

We want to be happy. We deserve to be happy. We can be happy if that's what we make up our minds to be.

My unhappiness can't be blamed on someone else. Immaturity makes me want to blame others, but my program friends won't let me get away with it. Today I will choose to be happy.

Expectations may set us up for disappointment.

Having expectations is not necessarily bad. We might be inspired to tackle worthy goals because of our expectations. But having too many expectations of others can lead to frustration, for them and for us.

When we dwell too much on our expectations, we aren't present to the reality of the moment. Our expectations, therefore, can cheat us of the journey God has designed for us. And by creating expectations of others, we deny that they have a right to their own perception of reality. When we expect them to do it our way, we are discounting them and their journeys. That's not on the agenda God has designed for us.

Are my expectations, for me or someone else, in my way today?

DECEMBER

For most of our lives, we have pushed or been pushed to persevere, to never give up trying to attain worthy goals. Thus learning now that we need to surrender to God's will seems counter to all that had helped us succeed in years past.

When doors are locked, look for the key.

SURRENDER

What we come to understand is that we need not give up our goals; indeed, we should strive to accomplish them. But when we find doors closing in our faces or get repeated rejections for our efforts, we need to look to our Higher Power for understanding. Perhaps our direction is not consistent with God's will. Surrendering, then, becomes the solution. And the right goal for us will emerge. Getting on track with God will assure us peaceful well-being.

Am I in tune with God's plan for me today?

Taking an honest inventory of our actions just before we go to sleep may reveal that we opened our mouth when it should have been closed. But it's not easy to be quiet when we are certain we are right. *After all, she shouldn't drink, should she? And if he keeps skipping out on work, he'll get fired.*

No matter how right we think we are, whether at work, in the grocery store, or at home, we have to let go of trying to direct the behavior of others. We have quite enough to handle just being in charge of ourselves.

What a gift this fellowship is! We never knew we could make a habit of keeping quiet.

In this fellowship, we are learning to keep an open mind and a closed mouth.

BEING QUIET

I will bite my tongue if I have to today, but I won't tell someone else what to do!

Accepting every experience as educational keeps us from feeling sorry for ourselves when our egos get pinched. We simply can't get through this life without experiencing situations we'd rather have avoided. However, placing a value judgment on which experiences are good for us and which aren't does no good. God is orchestrating our lives, and we do receive the education we need.

Feeling sorry for ourselves doesn't change anything.

DIFFICULTIES

Deciding that every experience can be interpreted as good is no more difficult than believing the cards are stacked against us. It's a matter of outlook, and no one controls it for us. We are in charge of our outlook. We can seek the humor or the lesson in situations, or we can feel victimized. We can't change the situation, but we can respond to it however we decide.

God is my instructor. And my lessons today aren't meant to hurt, ever, but to help me grow and change. I will trust them.

Learning comes from listening— to other people and to ourselves.

T? GOD'S PLAN

Our Higher Power speaks to us in so many ways. Some people believe that every conversation we have offers us messages from God. Wise philosophers from earlier centuries believed that every encounter we had with another person was *really* an encounter with some aspect of ourselves and that God brought us together for what we needed to learn.

In this program, we are given tools for listening to and sharing with others. And we are getting better at using these tools. Most of us have come to believe that's a gift from God.

Listening to others becomes a real joy, once we get free of our false pride that says we must have all the answers.

I can help someone today by sharing what I have learned from my Higher Power. I will keep learning if I keep listening.

It is hard indeed to let go of our feelings of anger, particularly when the addict in our life continues to use drugs. If we're patient, the program can help us accept that addiction is a disease. The addict didn't ask for it and doesn't want it but is powerless over its invasion. Our anger can't change that.

It never helps to be angry at the drug addict.

POWERLESSNESS

We too are powerless. We can't make the addict stop using chemicals. We can't make the disease go away. We can't stop the ramifications of continued use. We can't change anyone's life but our own. Still, this gives us the freedom from anger we need and deserve.

Before coming into the program, most of us didn't understand how futile and time-consuming anger was. We thought that if we got angry in the right way, we could make the alcoholic stop drinking. Repeatedly, however, we failed.

How good it feels to give up anger. It has given us back our lives.

I will live my life today and not let someone else's behavior steal my composure or my plan for the day.

To believe in change is half the battle.

We often focus on other people and the changes we want them to make. We might be convinced that if they changed, our behavior would too. But can we count on that? Some would say no, citing the old saying, "Wherever we go, there we are." Instead, we need to change our behavior specifically. We can never count on others' changing, but we can always count on our changing, if that's what we want.

Does it sound too easy? It's really not difficult as long as we honestly desire to change and then surrender to our Higher Power, who will help us believe that anything is possible. First we must consider what behavior we want to give up. Have we considered what behavior we might substitute for it? When we know both, we can proceed; however, we might not get far if we don't include God in the trip. The program promises that we can change. It's up to us to follow through.

I really can change any behavior I'm not proud of. Today is as good a day as any to start practicing new behavior.

Pouting and yelling over not getting our way are very common responses among family members of addicts. Seldom do the drinkers do what we want! Regardless of our reactions to them, they still do whatever they please. The time is right for us to focus on our own lives.

Nothing is gained by feeling ashamed of our defects.

If we were to take an honest inventory at this point in our development, we would find that not everything about us is good. And that's normal. But not everything about us is bad, either. We aren't always pouting and yelling. Often we are giving solace to others or laughing with friends. Generally, we follow through on tasks begun, and we are willing to change course as needed. Whoever we are at this moment is acceptable to our Higher Power. Who we become tomorrow is up to us.

We won't have to feel ashamed of our behavior if we take the time to choose how we really want to act. If we slip, we can always do it differently next time.

It's enough to focus only on my behavior today. An asset can be substituted for a defect before it's too late, and then no amends will be necessary.

Guidance doesn't always come in the way we expect.

Needing guidance is human, but many of us used to struggle against admitting that we didn't know how to proceed. Our dilemma was this: Asking other people for help made us feel inadequate. But when we didn't ask for help, our problems persisted.

Now we are learning that there are many safe ways to receive help. One of the easiest and least threatening is simply quieting our minds so that our Higher Power can be heard. Sometimes, however, we may hear our own egos instead, so we must be wary. Asking close friends for suggestions is another way our Higher Power can reach us. And again, we have to be certain we are open to *their* words, not to the words of our own egos.

A third way our Higher Power can reach us is through messages. We have heard from those wiser than we are that God's messages are everywhere. Perhaps we will find a message in the passages of a respected book. The point is that asking for help makes us ready to receive it. When our requests are sincere and our hearts humble, we'll gather the guidance we are ready for.

I will be open to the help I seek today.

If we'll let it, the Third Step of our program will change our lives in a most profound way. This Step asks us to turn our will over to *the care* of God. In other words, we need to do three things: (1) Give up control. (2) Give up worry. (3) Quiet our minds and listen to our inner voice. It's not impossible to do these things once we get accustomed to them, and they certainly take the guesswork out of what our response to any situation should be. We'll know what to do. And we'll see that God has every outcome under control.

We have spent so many fruitless hours worrying about other people and our relationships with them. We have felt compelled to force doors open, for them and for ourselves. We have driven people away because we have tried to play God in their lives—all because of worry. Give it up. Let God be God.

Worry means we aren't letting God do God's work.

T² STEP THREE

If I begin to worry today, I'll know I'm taking over for God. I can stop myself from worrying.

*Stop and
think...*

LETTING GO

RESTRAINT

T² THINK BEFORE
ACTING/TALKING

A good habit to develop is deciding to stop and think before reacting to an accusation or contrary opinion, or before taking action in any situation. Taking a few seconds to deliberately pause and quiet ourselves before speaking will keep us from complicating our relations with others.

The need to be right is human nature. But just because everyone struggles with this issue doesn't mean we should excuse it in ourselves. Pausing to ask ourselves, "Is this really worth arguing over?" will help most of us make the decision to back off, to let go, to choose peacefulness instead. Once we begin doing this regularly, we'll sense the power it gives us, power to decide who we will be every moment. Our confidence and self-worth will reflect this healthy empowerment. We'll never want to go back to our old ways.

I will begin the day with a quiet mind. I will go within before responding to others today.

Making the effort to be courteous is surprisingly easy once we conquer our initial resistance. It feels good to offer pleasing comments and smiles to friends and strangers alike. The unfamiliarity of courtesy and our fear that we'll be rebuffed make being courteous difficult at first.

Courtesy keeps our defects to a minimum.

Being courteous is a daily decision. And if we make this decision, in a very short time we'll have the privilege of discovering that the tension so common at work, at home, and with friends or family has dissipated. Initially, we think other people have changed. In reality, the change is in us. Courtesy has ushered in periods of serenity that we had not anticipated would come our way.

Why must courtesy be a learned behavior? Perhaps for some people it isn't, but many of us in recovery have dodged any behavior that makes us vulnerable. We played our cards close to avoid being taken advantage of. How much easier it is to relax and let courtesy reign.

My experiences today will reflect my willingness to treat everyone I meet courteously. It's within my power to be in charge of my day.

Resentments creep up on us. Where they come from isn't always evident. Some days it seems easier to feel resentful than to feel anything else. What is the payoff? There must be one, or we wouldn't harbor resentments with such relish.

Resentments indicate our attitude needs adjusting.

RESENTMENT

Doing a Fourth Step inventory will give us insight into our resentments. Not being able to control other people is an obvious trigger. Situations that begin to unfold according to someone else's plan rather than our own initiate resentment too. What it boils down to is, we get resentful when we don't get our way, which happens quite often.

Doing a Fifth Step next will help us appreciate how human it is to want to control. Yet what folly! We aren't in charge, God is. Working on acceptance every time we feel resentful will change the very flavor of our lives. In time our payoff will come from our happy attitude.

If I'm resentful today, I will remember God's role in my life and let the old anger go.

Most of us sought Twelve Step recovery because we were in pain. Whether we lived with a chemically dependent person or were on the ragged edge of life because of our obsession to control other people, we needed relief. The program is giving it to us. The equation, however, calls for us to do more than just be present at meetings. We need to take certain actions if we want long-term relief.

Changing our lives is a personal decision.

CHANGE

TO

STEPS

1, 2, 3

First, we have to admit we are *powerless* over other people. Regardless of our certainty that we are right, they must make their own decisions, pay their own consequences. Next, we have to believe in the possibility of God. When we have made that leap of faith, our obsession to control will be lessened. Third, we have to let this new God of our understanding take charge of our lives and our wills. When others say we are in good hands, we can trust that their words are true.

These first three Steps are only the beginning, but if we work these Steps, they promise monumental changes in our lives.

I didn't end up here because my life was wonderful, but I have the tools now to make it what I want. I'll use these tools today.

There is no <u>shame</u> in being chemically dependent.

Before getting involved in this program, most of us did not understand chemical dependency as a disease. We used shame and guilt, to no avail, to keep the alcoholic or other addict from drinking or drugging. We believed that the chemically dependent person's behavior reflected on us. We didn't want other people to judge us as unworthy just because of the alcoholic or other addict's behavior.

What we have learned from others in recovery has removed the stigma about the disease. Hearing an alcoholic say he or she is grateful to be one no longer surprises us, and we are becoming grateful too for the tools we are learning to use. Our lives are far saner since coming to believe there is a Power who watches over us, and nothing fills us with fear the way everything used to.

I am truly lucky. This disease has given me a rich and rewarding life. I'll share my good fortune with someone else today.

Twelve Step meetings seem to be a gathering place for the truly wise. We can't be sure at first what it is these people have, but we know we want it too.

We're all capable of possessing wisdom.

Attending meetings, reading Twelve Step literature, and choosing a sponsor who has a program we admire will change how we think and live daily. We'll learn, as our sponsors have learned before us, to keep our focus on the little things we can improve. We'll learn, as they have, to let go of others, letting God be in charge. We'll learn, as they have, to live just for today. And then we'll realize that we are beginning to have what these wise people have.

By following their example, we'll begin to appear wise, peaceful, and hopeful to newcomers. All of us can attain this quality if we really want it.

Today I can be as wise as the ones I admire. I now have a blueprint to follow. I'll start by keeping my focus small and my thinking simple.

Obsessing keeps us stuck and weakens our spirit.

INNER PEACE

SERENITY

We must give up trying to figure out other people. What they do is their journey, not ours. When we let their actions take up residence in our minds, we interrupt our own journey.

What we carry in our minds either nurtures us or tires us. We can be either refreshed or smothered by our thoughts. It's easy to forget that we can discard any thought we don't want. Our thoughts are not in charge of us; we are in charge of them!

Learning to quiet our minds will allow us the opportunity to feel the presence of our Higher Power. Getting quiet and going within will help us understand our personal journey and help us be willing to let others have theirs.

My own journey and relationship with my Higher Power are all that need to be on my mind today.

Prayer is often rote, lacking thought or meaning. Maybe as children we were scolded if we forgot to pray at mealtimes and at bedtime. In many homes, God is portrayed as the keeper of the black book that records our transgressions, not a friend who wants to help us.

Even though we're grown up now, we often carry with us our childlike interpretation of God. Learning to trust the God we hear about in the program takes effort. But the rewards are grand.

God will be a friend who will guide us in every endeavor if we'll suspend our resistance to the messages we receive: the words of loving friends; passages in a treasured book; specific suggestions from a trusted sponsor; the knowing that comes when we get quiet, *really quiet,* and listen to the urge within. Getting comfortable and relying on God will take the guesswork and the fear out of everyday happenings as well as traumatic ones. We will become the peaceful, serene people we've envied for years. All we have to do is change how we think about and pray to God.

Getting to know God changes us wholly.

T² GUIDANCE FROM GOD

I will look to God as my friend today, and my answers will come.

Alcoholism is an illness, not a judgment.

T² PROGRAM

It's not always easy to remember that our husband or daughter is sick when we are the butt of a cruel joke or the recipient of some other form of verbal abuse. Or worse. It's particularly difficult in the early months of our recovery. Nonetheless, we keep hearing that time and patience and listening to the wisdom of others will ease our pain and heighten our understanding. We are seeing that this is true.

No one asked for the disease of alcoholism. And we didn't intend to marry it or give birth to it. But it happened, just as cancer or depression happens. Over that part we are powerless.

Fortunately, we aren't powerless over our response. Being with other people who understand, sharing our experiences, extending a helping hand to newcomers, and letting the chemically dependent person run his or her own life make the real difference in how we feel each day.

I am grateful that I am in the caring community of a Twelve Step program. It is changing my life and my expectations of the future.

Only a very few families escape dysfunction. Relationship expert Virginia Satir has been credited with saying 98 percent of all families suffer from some dysfunction. How lucky for us, then, that so much help is available.

We are lucky indeed.

GRATITUDE

The founders of this Twelve Step program must have been inspired. How else could they have discovered the lifesaving force inherent in sharing one's story with another suffering soul? That two individuals came together and gave birth to this movement that has healed millions of people was God's will, without a doubt.

Being part of this movement means we have been chosen to carry on God's work. Keeping this in mind gives us a much better appreciation for the role alcoholism has played in our families and among our friends. We are lucky indeed. We are healing. And we are helping others to heal.

I will be grateful today for all the help available. I am part of God's plan to heal others.

How we treat other people comes back to us— always.

Offering others understanding and compassion changes how we perceive the world around us on a daily basis. Our acts of love inspire love from others. What we send out to the people who share our path changes, ever so subtly, the complexion of each life we touch. In fact, the whole world is changed by even the tiniest of acts.

The simple truth is, our own attitudes often determine what kind of experiences we'll have. Anger and resentment won't bring us peace. Suspicion and accusation will backfire. Most of us have tried to control all the people and all the experiences in our lives. And we have failed. Now we are realizing that the love that comes back to us is the love that we express.

I will feel love today from at least one person if I offer it to many.

Step One says, "We admitted we were powerless over alcohol—that our lives had become unmanageable." This Step is difficult for us. After all, we think, alcohol isn't our problem, it's the alcoholic's.

Powerlessness is at first hard to understand.

We like to control. We like to manage. We resist admitting we aren't able to make others do as we wish. And we abhor the idea that our lives are "unmanageable." But there is hope for us. Given enough time, we'll begin to see how the First Step applies to our lives.

Reflection on the earlier years might help us remember how seldom we succeeded at getting other people to do our will. We tried, incessantly no doubt, and failed. How many situations turned into crises because we were "overmanaging" the outcomes? We filled our days with the behavior and the concerns of others. The details that were clearly ours to handle often got lost in the chaos.

The Twelve Step program can give us relief. With effort, we'll admit we're powerless. And as the idea grows in us, we'll even begin to love that we're powerless. Our burdens will be lifted as if by magic.

I will be grateful that I'm in control of no one but myself today.

Our Higher Power loves us unconditionally.

What is unconditional love? Not being able to explain what it is or how it might feel is typical. It's certainly not unusual to have grown up in homes where love was expressed only in response to high grades or the completion of chores. Being loved for *just being* is not a common memory for many of us.

Hearing from others in the group that they and God love us in spite of our defects is not very believable at first. Since childhood we have known we aren't perfect, and thus we feel unlovable.

Time will help us believe we are loved. Being surrounded by friends who express their love to us will help us believe. And the healing will come. The best result of believing in the possibility of unconditional love is that we'll be able to feel it for others too.

My Higher Power loves me fully today. Even if I fail to live up to my expectations, I will have lived up to God's. Meditating on this will help me believe it.

Most of us used to feel desperate, overwhelmed with fear, about our lives or someone else's life. Our worry was incessant, and we doubted we'd ever be free of it. But the darkness began to recede when people in the program shared how they had handled a similar situation. Hearing that traumatic times are survivable gives us the strength to continue our journey. From other voices we hear hope, and we realize that we'll be okay.

Giving away what we have learned continues the miracle of hope. In this way we are the keepers of our brothers and sisters. Making the journey smoother for someone else lightens our own struggle every day.

Sharing our experiences with other people gives them hope.

EXPERIENCE
LESSONS

Helping someone by sharing a part of my life today will help me remember the lessons I have learned.

It's harmful to feel inferior or superior to other people.

INFERIORITY
SUPERIORITY

Coming to believe that we are equal to the people who share our lives each day and to the other men and women we meet by happenstance—this is an important gift of the Twelve Step program. Most of us, however, have had to work at self-acceptance. Comparing ourselves to others became an obsession, and every glance at someone else became a time of evaluation: Were we the winners or the losers?

Knowing that each of us has a special role to play in the life of *every person* we'll meet today is profoundly valuable. We will not be drawn into making comparisons. We'll not need to feel either inferior or superior. We can be restful, knowing that we can contribute to the world as we are. Our gifts are unique and needed by the people with us right now.

I will be aware of my gifts to others today. I am what is needed.

When our children or our friends look to us for guidance, we feel compelled to offer suggestions honestly and lovingly, and we hope we can help them. We want their lives to be peaceful and successful. Why should it be any different when we look to our Higher Power for guidance? God's role is as a loving friend or parent. And we will know how to handle situations that used to baffle us if we let God's guidance into our lives.

Guidance is a gift we can expect when we turn to our Higher Power.

T2 Promise #11   GUIDANCE FROM GOD

What a relief to know that we don't have to struggle with difficult situations by ourselves anymore. The decision to leave a relationship, switch jobs, move, or confront a friend no longer has to be made by us alone. A short prayer followed by quiet meditation T2 will inform us of the action to take. If no answer seems to come, we can trust that right now is not the time for action. God's timetable may not be the same as ours. Let's be patient.

I will be more serene today if I follow the guidance that comes to me through prayer and meditation.

DECEMBER 26

Friendships divide our burdens and double our joys.

T? SHARING

Having women and men we trust enough to share our deepest secrets with is one of the many gifts of the program. While it's true that most of us already had friends, we seldom told them everything about ourselves. We held back the most intimate details to protect ourselves. We thought if they really knew us, they'd never want to be our friends.

Our understanding of friendship has changed since being introduced to the Twelve Steps. How we act as friends has changed too. Now we know that friends don't judge, they don't try to control, they accept how other people are, and they never betray a confidence. They listen, they love, and they offer hope. And they don't run away when they don't like what they hear. What we have learned influences our old friendships too, and everybody benefits.

To express my friendship fully to someone today means sharing honestly what I'm experiencing and listening intently while my friend shares too.